Computer-Based Reference Service

Computer-Based Reference Service

M. Lorraine Mathies
and Peter G. Watson

American Library Association

Chicago 1973

Library of Congress Cataloging in Publication Data

Mathies, Lorraine
  Computer-based reference service

  Bibliography: p.
  1. Information storage and retrieval systems.
2. Libraries—Automation. I. Watson, Peter G.,
joint author. II. Title.
Z699.M36   029.5   73–9967
ISBN 0–8389–0156–5

Contents

part one

ERIC: A Model Information System

v

Figures

Foreword

Computer-Based Reference Service is the outgrowth of a program which began at the 1968 Annual Conference of the American Library Association held in Atlantic City. At that conference the Information Retrieval Committee of the Reference Services Division discussed at considerable length the growing gap between that small elite in the library world who were involved with computers and the great mass of the nation's professional librarians who were essentially intimidated by these electronic tools. A number of ideas were put forth which gradually coalesced into the concept of an ALA preconference, aimed at presenting to working reference librarians the essentials of the reference potential of computers and the machine-readable data they produce.

Because such a meeting could only reach a small fraction of the profession, it was assumed from the start that both the format of the meeting and the instructional materials prepared for it should be so designed that the program could be effectively repeated on a local or regional basis.

An initial proposal, drafted in large part by Barbara Markuson, was submitted to the RSD Board by the committee at the January 1970 Midwinter Meeting in Chicago. The board approved the proposal and authorized the creation of a special subcommittee to draft a more detailed plan for submission to the Dallas Conference Planning Committee. This was done at the 1970 Annual Conference in Detroit, when the search for appropriate personnel to prepare the necessary materials, schedules, and other details was begun.

A special meeting of the Planning Subcommittee established a budget and made the decision to utilize the services of Peter Watson, who has had experience in a similar type of venture within the UCLA Library system. At this meeting the subcommittee also made the critical decision to use essentially one data base for purposes of instruction, selecting the ERIC system. ERIC was chosen as the model system because searches of this file require relatively little in the way of a specialized background and vocabulary to be understandable to the novice. Hence the exemplary use of ERIC, it was supposed, would produce minimal distraction from the main objectives of understanding computer-based reference systems and of acquiring basic skills in the techniques of effective computer search and manipulation.

Peter Watson enlisted the aid of Dr. M. Lorraine Mathies who has had extensive experience with ERIC, and together they undertook to produce a manual and workbook for the tutorials which were the core of the preconference. Details were completed at the 1971 Midwinter Meeting in Los Angeles.

The Preconference [on] Computer-Based Reference Service was, in the opinion of most of the participants, an educational success, and the Information Retrieval Committee moved promptly to arrange for publication of the tutor's manual, because a published version was thought to be critical for the projected regional and local meetings envisioned as the means of reaching a significantly larger segment of the profession. A number of suggestions for revision were made by ALA Publishing Services. The authors agreed to undertake the requested revisions, and, in the process, made several significant changes of their own, with the result that they have produced what the committee believes will prove to be a substantially more valuable work. The components have been regrouped into a more coherent whole, and, although ERIC is still the basic system used, additional attention has been given to twelve other data bases, with especial attention to MARC and the 1970 census tapes.

It would be impossible in the space available to give full credit to all of the planners of the preconference, whose skilled and enthusiastic contributions made it work, or to all of the members of the two committees and the dedicated ALA staff personnel whose efforts made it possible. However, I would be remiss if I did not at least mention the two RSD presidents, Dean Margaret Goggin, whose vision recognized the potential value of the project, and John McGowan, whose drive and organizing ability were major factors in converting dream into reality.

University of Toledo
Toledo, Ohio

JOHN M. MORGAN
Reference Librarian
University Libraries
and Associate Professor
of Library Administration

Acknowledgments

It is a pleasure to record our appreciation for the indispensable help we received in the preparation of this book.

Data on the ERIC information system was derived from several sources, primarily the *ERIC Operating Manual* and the *Thesaurus of ERIC Descriptors*. Permission to use these was granted by Charles Hoover, Chief of ERIC, and William Burgess, Vice President, Macmillan Corporation. In addition, W. Ted Brandhorst, Director of the ERIC Processing and Reference Facility of LEASCO Systems and Research Corporation, provided many helpful comments on the original preconference manuscript.

For their able assistance with the manuscript, we would like to thank Sue Ann Power, Aeint de Boer, Alison Watson, and Elizabeth Dixon. For their guidance in the actual publication, we are pleased to acknowledge the help of the ALA Editorial staff, namely Richard Gray, Sylvia Royt, and Helen Cline. Finally, we are grateful to Marian Ellithorpe and Judia Campbell for their expert typing.

University of California   M. LORRAINE MATHIES
Los Angeles   Head, Education and Psychology Library

    PETER G. WATSON
    Head, Center for Information Services
    University Research Library

Introduction

Modern society incessantly produces and uses information. For decades librarians have acted as "keepers" or "guardians" of these accumulated efforts, only to find their shelves becoming choked with a proliferation of publications and their users sometimes stunned by the delays in moving a book from one reader to another. The need for a device or mechanism to transport and filter information into a format which is adaptable to a variety of interests and usable in a multitude of situations seems so obvious that to mention it is redundant. It is in this environment that the digital computer, with its new technologies, has become of primary concern to librarians.

In recent years a new concept which one might call the "information resources market" has appeared on the information scene. Its constituents are composed of sellers, such as professional societies and commercial organizations offering computer-readable data, often with "tailor-made" services, and buyers, such as libraries and information centers seeking answers to the diverse needs of their clientele through the use of automated resources. The subject areas covered by these data files, the type and depth of indexing, the number of retrieval points—these and other characteristics of such data bases have now become an important aspect of the librarian's responsibility to communicate with his patrons. No matter what the setting may be—whether in a small college, a remote public library, or even a large academic institution—librarians must be versatile in discussing these so-called nonconventional ways of processing and retrieving information.

Librarians have long served the information needs of the community. And, as Hayes and Becker indicate, the principal library functions of acquisitions, cataloging, storage, and circulation apply to automated data bases as well:

> The emphasis on indexing rather than cataloging, dissemination rather than circulation, brings out the special attributes of a computer-based system . . . while circulation suggests a reader taking a book out of a library, dissemination includes both this and active transmission of the contents to a reader at a remote console. Cataloging suggests the standard author, title, and subject guides. Indexing includes not only these, but greater depth of detail as well, through the ability of computer programs quickly to process vast amounts of data according to detailed and complex instructions.[1]

It is in this spirit that this book, which was derived from a manual prepared for an ALA Preconference on Computer-Based Reference Service in 1971, is presented. It is arranged in three sections following that of the Preconference Tutorials, although the substance has been pervasively revised.

Librarians are known as traditionalists and as innovators; mechanized information services are in need of both. The subjects covered by automated data bases span nearly the entire range of scientific knowledge and extend into the humanities and social sciences, although coverage is not equally balanced from subject to subject. Some tape services provide broad, interdisciplinary coverage; others, such as the ERICTAPES, are concerned with providing coverage of the various aspects of a given discipline. A large portion of these data bases is devoted to the coverage of journal literature, both comprehensively and selectively. Others are concerned with monographs, reports, theses, patents, newspapers, and even private information sources. The range of variety and scope of these mechanized information services is steadily increasing, and an understanding of the principles of this form of information control is essential for the contemporary librarian.

An Example of a Computerized
Information Retrieval System

Of the numerous files of computer-readable information that are available, two data bases unique to the field of education were selected for this publication as being typical examples of the ways in which information is acquired, processed, and otherwise prepared for retrieval and use. These data bases, *Research in Education* (hereinafter referred to as RIE) and the *Current Index to Journals in Education* (hereinafter referred to as CIJE) are illustrative of computer-produced, serial bibliographies. They serve primarily as indexes to the fugitive report literature and journal articles in the field of education. Both are the products of a federally sponsored, decentralized information network, known as the Educational Resources Information Center (hereinafter referred to as ERIC).

RIE and CIJE provide many of the basic characteristics of an automated information retrieval system. The acquisition of documents and the conditions of their acceptance, the development and control of the language of the field, and the indexing of this input—all are representative ways of preparing and retrieving information for users of libraries and information centers.

The Computer and Information Retrieval: Some Guidelines

The computer is a most powerful tool for the fast handling of large quantities of information, but the notion that it is capable of assuming *all* library functions, thus rendering libraries obsolete, was never given much credence by those acquainted with libraries at the operational level. This is as true of a library's technical processing tasks as it is of its public service responsibilities, which are the primary concern here. To be specific, the computer will not display its full advantage if it is matched against a single, straightforward request that may be searched manually. For example, if one wants only to see what is listed under "JUNIOR COLLEGES" in the latest issue of RIE (the ERIC abstract journal), the most efficient way is undoubtedly the conventional one: go to the journal, look in the index, and, if appropriate, photocopy a page or two of the journal. Under what circumstances, then, is this elaborate searching method really beneficial in terms of time, cost, and thoroughness? Following are some of the typical conditions whose occurrence may alert the reference librarian to the possibility of authorizing a computer search, a situation which will no doubt become increasingly widespread during the next few years.

1. *Multidimensional Searches.* Requests involving anything from five to forty terms (more terms than can reasonably be held in the mind while carrying out a manual search) are regarded as typical of most present-day computer searches. These can be drawn from any element of data within a record that the computer programs can manipulate, and can also then be combined into several logical configurations by means of Boolean strategy, weighting, or other search techniques.

2. *Large Files.* Since one of the primary motivations for putting any data file into machine-readable form is the modern need to control exponentially growing amounts of data, bibliographic reference files in this medium are either already very large or are intended to grow rapidly to a substantial size. Thus, any request where the size of the file to be searched is in the tens or hundreds of thousands of citations is a potential candidate for employment of the computer.

3. *Literature Searches in Science and Technology.* The factors previously mentioned are presently found to be more characteristic of science and technology, including medicine, than of the humanities and social sciences. It is here that the "information explosion" has so far been most evident, although there are many signs to indicate that the social sciences are undergoing an information explosion of their own. For instance, beginning in 1970, approximately thirty times as much census data will be available on magnetic tape from each decennial census as will be found in printed volumes. This is a remarkable example of the mounting information problem in the social sciences.

4. *Knowledge in New Patterns.* Whatever the discipline, computerized searching will more and more become a tool for those working with new configurations of knowledge in the future. Because it provides the capability for doing highly complex searches organized on any of the fields in a record and on massive quantities of data, machine searching will foster the extraction of information in new patterns, rather than merely being a quicker way of performing traditional search processes. Naturally, this applies to whatever type of information is made machine-readable—whether bibliographic citations, summary statistics or raw numerical data, or full prose texts.

5. *Multiple Searches.* The machine search can be a remarkably efficient way of fulfilling the requests of many patrons in one operation. Obviously, this type of reference assistance was a part of library service long before computers. For example, college librarians for years have utilized numerous special procedures to deal with "crash" demands upon the same few textbooks or bibliographies. But it seems apparent that the particular qualities of speed and accuracy, areas where the computer is spectacularly efficient, will enable it to extend this capability of librarians manyfold, and thus place in their hands the means of greatly enhanced service. This can apply both to situations where the need is for multiple copies of the same output (one search printed many times) and, of far greater importance, where the need is for many customized searches of the same data file. Performance of several hundred different, complex, and individually tailored searches simultaneously is already routine at many information centers. In any case, the file is passed through the computer only one time.

Modes of Searching

There are two major types of bibliographic searching, each of which, though using the same basic techniques, possesses its own characteristics. To initiate a search, take as a framework a serially produced bibliographic file, such as RIE, and assume that the entire data base has been ordered. The first item to be received should be the back file, in this case from November 1966 to date; later, smaller sections of the file, the current issues or "update tapes," are delivered at regular intervals. It can be projected that a user may ask for one extensive retrospective search initially, to be followed by regular current searches of the update tapes, either on one specified topic, or perhaps several. If a patron has several distinct, unrelated areas of interest, those topics should be treated as individual searches; trying to combine different topics into one gigantic Boolean expression does not work.

1. *Retrospective Searching.* This type of searching is aimed primarily at exploiting the ability of the computer to run through enormous quantities of data at high speed. Although few files yet contain more than ten years of retrospective data (MEDLARS and *Science Citation Index* being among the oldest and the largest), considerable savings of personal bibliographic "legwork" are already possible, given a good searching system. By this is meant a set of processing programs which combine searching flexibility with machine efficiency. Generally, the large-scale retrospective search will be a one-time request, requiring careful coordination with the patron beforehand, so as to attain completeness and as much relevance as possible. As a matter of efficiency and economy, it is recommended that preliminary trial runs be made on an update tape or a test tape to check the actual effectiveness of the search statement. The typical retrospective request will be for a search on one or more of the main bibliographic elements in the record, such as author, title, or subject, although other fields also may be examined.

The present costs of a retrospective search will almost certainly strike any librarian as fearfully high. (In this instance, the term "cost" is used only in the narrow, technical sense of "costs in computer time.") Therefore it is important to spend considerable time preparing the search statement in advance. For example, it is not unusual for a single search covering three or four years of a file to cost $300 to $400. Any such search obtained for under $100 is certainly low-priced by present standards. However, it must be immediately clear that such costs are a factor of two things: the operating efficiency of the computer programs and the formula by which the computer center charges for machine time. The same search will undoubtedly cost widely differing amounts in different locations or under different programming operations. Since costs of computer time are falling steadily and experience in programming is increasing rapidly, the same search will certainly be far less expensive in five years than it is at present. Techniques for overcoming this large outlay in search time and money are increasingly being brought into operation. In one respect, these procedures do exactly what a human does in attacking a major bibliographic search, that is, use indexes to the main file as screening mechanisms. Another tactic for reducing the costs of retrospective searching is to use "batch processing," whereby a number of transactions or searches to be processed are accumulated and processed simultaneously, thus reducing the cost to each user.

A possible complication with the procedure of retrospective searching arises after several update tapes have been received. This stems from the fact that it costs money to merge these recent segments into the master file. However, if this is not done, a retrospective search comes to involve much extra time and the additional trouble of needing to have many tape reels mounted and searched individually.

2. *Current Searching.* As early as 1958, Hans Peter Luhn saw the pattern of service that must logically emerge from the advent of computerized information.[2] Like most genuine discoveries, it was a blend of existing knowledge, common sense, and imagination. It is the technique called "Selective Dissemination of Information" (SDI), one of the most widely discussed and extensively tested developments to appear so far in information science. The element of existing knowledge is the basic, typical search strategy for extracting information from mechanized files, as discussed above. The patron states his information needs primarily in terms of subject requirements, but allowing, where necessary, searches for specific authors, years of publication, and the like. When properly coded, this request is run against the file; anything which matches it is retrieved. If the data base is a serial publication, such as the mechanized version of an abstracting and indexing periodical, the patron can return a month or so later and submit the same set of requirements. For this purpose, it is only necessary to search the current tape; but if the patron is going to ask for the same search to be made upon each incoming update tape, it is immediately clear that he may as well leave his request on file with the library reference or information center and have the output sent to his office regularly. The patron is thus automatically notified of new material which is potentially significant to him. This calls for the formulation of a *profile* of the patron's permanent subject interests which itself can be stored in machine-readable form. In this way, a file of such user-interest profiles can be established, and each incoming tape need only be run against that file one time. F. Wilfrid Lancaster, in his *Information Retrieval Systems,* has characterized the reversal in search technique that has occurred:

The principal distinction between SDI and retrospective searching systems is that in the case of the latter, a user request precipitates a search of a document file, whereas, in the former, a document precipitates a search of a user file.[3]

Furthermore, the all-important element of feedback can now be introduced with the purpose of system improvement. Depending upon how well a given search satisfies the client, he can modify his profile, thus progressively improving the response from the information retrieval system until a satisfactory combination is achieved between the number of documents *recalled* and the *precision* (accuracy) of those retrieved.

SDI actually formalizes a particular area of reference service and renders it machine-manipulable. This has two very significant effects: first, it vastly increases the scale on which such individually tailored requests can be undertaken by an already busy library; and second, it permits many refinements in the scope of such service. The librarian, no less than the scholar, has long wished that the library could find it economically feasible to provide greater depth of subject access to monographs, journal articles, reports, and other fugitive literature and to the serial bibliographies that cover them. Even the tasks of charging SDI searches to their respective requesters, maintaining current accounts for each patron, addressing the output for mailing, and keeping detailed usage statistics can be handled by the computer. However, such concepts regarding the dissemination of information presuppose that librarians see their role not merely as that of a preserver of records, but more importantly as that of a specialist in the transmission of information to those who need it. To coin a comparison not intended as unfavorable to either party, the librarian must see his function more in terms of a merchandizer who sends his product out on approval, knowing that a certain percentage of sales will cover the cost of mailing the item to those who will not want it. In the same way, it is probable, obviously, that the library's early attempts at regularly and automatically disseminating information to many clients at once will result in a percentage of failures. It is, however, clearly better that the library should make such efforts, rather than wait for its patrons to create a demand for a new type of information service.

Each year sees growing throngs of people needing more information— and needing it faster and in increasingly sophisticated configurations. They especially need better information and service in the intermediate tasks of getting to the documents which they are ultimately seeking. Putting current serial bibliographies and other information into computer-readable form is intended to assist in this very crucial area of reference service. The data bases are there, and if the librarian declines to use them to help his clientele, there is little doubt that the client will go to where they are available. The librarian's professional role will thereafter be gradually redefined more narrowly, into an archivist, a keeper of print. We prefer to believe that the librarian's true function is that of a specialist in the handling of that elusive, yet critical commodity, information.

Notes

1. Robert M. Hayes and Joseph Becker, *Handbook of Data Processing* (New York: Wiley, 1971), p. 697.
2. Hans Peter Luhn, "A Business Intelligence System," *IBM Journal of Research and Development* 2(4): 314–19 (Oct. 1958).
3. F. Wilfrid Lancaster, *Information Retrieval Systems* (New York: Wiley, 1968), p. 53.

ERIC: A Model Information System

1

Information Flow through the ERIC System

In recent years, the information resources market has seen the development of an increasing amount of computer-readable data, particularly in the format of bibliographic information. At least two such tape services are currently offered directly through federal agencies: *ERICTAPES,* through the Educational Resources Information Center, and *Government Reports Announcements,* from the National Technical Information Service. Numerous others are available through a variety of professional, scientific, technical, and commercial agencies. Since knowledge of the structure and manipulation of such files has become essential for librarians, the ERIC data base has been selected as an example of one method used to bring information control to a rapidly expanding, multidisciplinary field.

Introduction

The development of a literature of American education received its greatest impetus during the past fifteen years. This may be traced to a variety of happenings as, for example, the impact of Sputnik in 1957, with resulting public demands for more scientific and technological advances. It may also derive from a newly aroused concern for different life styles,

11

and the consequent pressures for social reform. Whatever the reasons and events that prompted massive study and analysis of educational matters, however, the results have produced a startling proliferation of the literature of educational research, and its management and relevance have become matters of crucial importance.

The so-called knowledge explosion in education has developed not only from increased public attention and support, but also from considerable progress in refining and streamlining the methodology of educational research. For example, interest in both the educational and other handicaps of disadvantaged children in rural and urban communities prompted the development of "Project Beacon" at Yeshiva University in 1961. Later, the College Entrance Examination Board helped to establish and support the Information Retrieval Center on the Disadvantaged (IRCD) at the same institution, and in 1964 the center's staff began to collect both published and unpublished documents relating to the disadvantaged. By 1965, the first *IRCD Bulletin* announcing the services of the center and reporting the findings of certain studies in its files had been published. In June 1966, the Information Retrieval Center on the Disadvantaged became the first clearinghouse in the ERIC network.

The "knowledge explosion" in education might better be described as a "literature explosion," since the scatter and volume of findings and reports have permeated all forms of both published and fugitive materials. The production of new journal titles, for example, has more than tripled. Federal support of research efforts has produced, among others, the "Cooperative Research Reports" and "Pacesetters in Innovation"; philanthropic concern has resulted in consortia, networks, institutes, and a variety of other innovative programs. Local and state school systems have initiated studies of their own resources and programs and, as a result, many have "regrouped" so as to improve their performances. Perhaps it was inevitable that the combination of these efforts would actually expand the scope of this rather imprecise body of knowledge to the extent that education has now become multidisciplinary both in derivation and coverage, with the resulting literature tending to contain some inconclusive or contradictory findings, repetitive writings, and even false knowledge.

Regardless of its characteristics, however, if a body of knowledge is to be useful, it must be subjected to scrutiny, and perhaps even be "repackaged" in the form of literature reviews or "state of the art" reports; its relevance or appropriateness to a variety of audiences must also be considered. Furthermore, a body of knowledge or information must be accessible to the potential user. Since 1929, the *Education Index* has served as a subject index and guide to a selected list of educational periodicals, conference proceedings, and yearbooks. From 1929 to 1961, the *Index* listed nearly all current references to the significant American (and some

British) sources by author and subject. After 1961, and until mid-1969, the *Index* discontinued the indexing of books, book reviews, research reports, government documents, courses of study, and other monographic publications. No author indexing was included, and the *Education Index* became primarily a subject index of the periodical literature in the field.

The headings or subjects used in describing materials for the *Index* have, for the most part, been standard *Library of Congress Subject Headings,* and as such they reflect the problems inherent in the maintenance of subject authority systems in large libraries. Subject headings identify concepts, and as the language of a literature changes, so should the topics or headings used to describe it. "Infantile Paralysis," for example, has given way to "Poliomyelitis," and "Tuberculosis" has outmoded "Consumption." Furthermore, the very structure of a large and highly complex subject list, with its predetermined subdivisions and preestablished subject combinations, makes it very difficult to allow for changes reflecting contemporary points of view. Therefore, from the user's point of view, the subject headings in the *Education Index* offer limited opportunities to search for current or broad interdisciplinary topics, and the results are often time-consuming and ineffective.

Thus, at a time of growing concern regarding the utilization and implementation of research results and other project-generated information, the flow of information from the producer to the user had been relatively low. There had been no systematic, nationwide plan for the acquisition, analysis, or dissemination of information. Nor had there been a satisfactory key to the literature of education, whether in the form of a well-developed, standardized vocabulary or a single, authoritative source of bibliographic control. This was the state of information control in the field of education in the mid-1960s.

The Educational Resources Information Center (ERIC)

ERIC is a national, decentralized, information system designed and developed by the U.S. Office of Education; it is now operated by the National Institute of Education (NIE). Originally organized as a program of the Bureau of Research, ERIC began with the support of education for the disadvantaged under the Elementary and Secondary Education Act of 1965. A preliminary effort involved the organization and dissemination of what has become known as the "Disadvantaged Collection" of 1,740 documents to the various state educational agencies and to certain local school districts. By 1966, four major objectives had been developed for the ERIC program:

To make unavailable or hard-to-find-but-significant research and research-related reports, papers, and documents easily available to the educational community.

To prepare interpretive summaries of information from many reports for use by educational decision-makers and practitioners.

To strengthen existing educational research dissemination channels.

To provide a base for developing a national education information network that can effectively link knowledge producers and users in education.[1]

Actually, ERIC should most appropriately be regarded as a system which is *one* program among the several dissemination and utilization efforts of the National Institute of Education (NIE). Although it may seem somewhat nebulous, ERIC's history can be dated from the establishment of the original components of the system. The Autonetics Division of North American Rockwell was the first large-scale contractor assigned to develop and implement the technical services aspects of the plan; this included the documentation activities, the development of a thesaurus of educational terminology, and the establishment of computerized retrieval services. That contract was signed in May 1966, and from February through June of that year, the first twelve clearinghouses were established. The distribution of documents, either in microfiche or hard copy, has also been handled by private enterprise. The initial contract for the ERIC Document Reproduction Service (EDRS) was awarded to the Bell and Howell Company in 1965. The Panel on Education Terminology (PET) was organized in 1966 to provide assistance in developing the *Thesaurus of ERIC* Descriptors. The first issue of *Research in Education,* a monthly abstract and index bulletin, was published in November 1966. Under federal government procurement regulations, new bids for operating the ERIC Document Reproduction Service were requested in September 1967. The successful bidder at that time was the National Cash Register Company. Recently, this contract has been awarded to LEASCO Information Products Company (LIPCO).

While ERIC has many features in common with other large national information systems, it has certain unique characteristics which set it apart. These include the broad range of sources from which documentary materials are acquired, the diverse interests and needs of the audiences to be served, the concept of a decentralized information system, and the principle of central lexicographic control with clearinghouse participation. The use of subject specialists, working in their own professional environments while performing documentation functions, is the key to the unique strengths, as well as to certain difficulties, in the ERIC system.

Currently, the ERIC system consists of six interrelated components:

A headquarters staff (Central ERIC), located in the National Institute of Education in Washington, D.C., provides overall management, policy, and technical direction for the system. Central ERIC also acquires U.S. Office of Education reports, as well as educational documents from other governmental agencies and departments, which are then distributed for processing to the appropriate components in the ERIC system.

A network of specialized, subject-oriented clearinghouses, located at various universities and professional organizations, performs documentation and information analysis functions.

A private contractor operates the ERIC Processing and Reference Facility, which provides centralized computer and other technical services, particularly in developing the tape version of RIE.

The U.S. Government Printing Office is the printer and distributor of RIE.

Macmillan Information is the publisher of *Current Index to Journals in Education* and other basic ERIC products, such as the *Thesaurus of ERIC Descriptors* and the *ERIC Educational Documents Index, 1966–1969*.

The ERIC Document Reproduction Service, operated by a private contractor, reproduces and sells the reports cited in RIE, either in microfiche or facsimile hardcopy.

Again, it is important to emphasize the fact that the ERIC system is regarded here as a representative example of automated bibliographic services, and, therefore, major attention will be given only to those components which either coincide with typical library practices or are representative of different concepts in information control.

ERIC Clearinghouses: Their Purpose and Structure

As indicated earlier, one of the unique features of the ERIC program may be found in its blend of the traditional aspects of centralized information storage and retrieval with a national, decentralized network of specialized information centers, such as the ERIC Clearinghouse on Urban Disadvantaged and the ERIC Clearinghouse on Educational Media and Technology. The ERIC response to the problem of incorporating high-level, professional subject competence into information management is to maintain subject-oriented experts in their preestablished environments, while they concurrently apply their knowledge and skills to the functions of clearinghouses located at their own institutions. In this way, the documentation activities of these professionals act as adjuncts to their primary career intentions, rather than as distractions to their personal progress.

Another factor which argues for the location of documentation activities at centers with established subject competencies is the fact that, generally, these centers have either amassed sizeable, specialized document collections for study, or they have access to the resources of large academic libraries. Furthermore, as leading professionals in their specialized fields, clearinghouse directors stimulate arrangements for the secondary dissemination of information through journals and other media of professional organizations. In addition, various interfaces are developed between ERIC and the professional areas of education represented by clearinghouses on the basis of the professional interests and needs of clearinghouse directors and officers of professional associations, editors of journals, chairmen of national conferences, and the like. Thus, the decentralized clearinghouse concept allows the ERIC system to build upon established communication patterns in education, and it permits quick, flexible action in constructing dissemination programs.

The structure of the clearinghouse component in the ERIC program is designed to achieve maximum coverage of the educational literature at the lowest reasonable costs. The selection of coverage for the major topical fields and problem areas in education is a matter of continuing review. Since the initial establishment of clearinghouses in 1966, a limited number of these centers have been added to the program, while others have been dropped or combined with existing units. Each clearinghouse focuses upon a major educational field or topic, and is responsible for monitoring, acquiring, evaluating, abstracting, and indexing reports for dissemination in ERIC products. In order to organize an effective strategy for collecting and disseminating appropriate and relevant information, and to reduce the amount of duplicative effort, each clearinghouse director has prepared a "scope note" delineating the scope and functions of his unit. Two examples follow:

ERIC CLEARINGHOUSE ON LIBRARY AND INFORMATION SCIENCES

Abstract of Scope:

Libraries, archives, information centers, information analysis centers; publishing industry; national libraries; librarians, information specialists and information scientists; library organizations; library training education and library schools; information science; information processing; information retrieval; library technology; management, operation and use of libraries and library facilities; library materials and equipment; related terminology and standards; information utilization and transfer; library and information systems and services; documentation.[2]

ERIC CLEARINGHOUSE ON COUNSELING AND PERSONNEL SERVICES

Abstract of Scope:

Counselors and personnel workers, their preparation, training, practice, and supervision at all educational levels and in all settings; the use and results of personnel procedures such as testing, interviewing, group work, case work, and the analysis of the resultant information relating to the individual and his environment; the theoretical development of counseling and guidance; the nature of pupil, student, and adult characteristics; descriptions of educational, occupational, and community settings; the types of assistance provided by personnel workers in such areas as career planning, family consultations, and student orientation activities, drug abuse, problems of aging.[3]

The Knowledge Linker

The retrieval of documents is only the first step in the application of information. In order for information to be useful to a wide audience in education, the data, theories, and generalizations often must be "repackaged" into interpretive summaries, literature reviews, or other formats. These information analysis products reach users in a variety of ways. Some are reproduced and disseminated by clearinghouses to a select audience. In other instances, clearinghouses generate original documents and then turn them over to professional organizations for final editing, printing, and sales. All documents of this type are cited in RIE and are available through the ERIC Document Reproduction Service. Clearinghouse products include newsletters, interpretive reports, and summaries which are often done in a monographic format.

The role of clearinghouse directors, in establishing relationships with the staffs of professional organizations and various governmental education agencies, has been mentioned previously. This role of "knowledge-linker" is of sufficient importance to warrant further discussion. In the development of educational and other types of research, it is seldom that "the producer of a bit of knowledge is responsible for inserting it in and propelling it through the 'knowledge-flow system.' "[4] The practicalities essential to the utilization of new knowledge often are not clearly understood by the producer, nor are the appropriate applications of theoretical concepts necessarily familiar to the professional practitioner. Administrators and superintendents at all levels—consultants, teachers, parents, and even students—all are members of an extensive audience through which the educational ideas and practices must filter. It seems obvious that, for the most part, their understanding and appreciation of the rigors and motivations of researchers are, at best, limited. Therefore, the role of an intermediary, or "linker-of-knowledge," becomes crucial to the efficient utilization or consumption of information. Furthermore, the channels of communication between the "producers-" and "users-of-information" are often so remote that contact is limited and vague.

In his efforts to reach such an audience, the knowledge-linker has a variety of channels from which to choose. In the ERIC program, linkage arrangements are available at the clearinghouse level through newsletters, regular columns in specialized professional journals, close relationships with professional organizations including presentations and demonstrations at conferences and conventions, cooperation in joint publication efforts, the development of formal liaison relationships with state education agencies, the support of training institutes and seminars, and, above all, direct service to educators. In this regard, if the role of a "knowledge-linker" is defined as an intermediary between two or more systems necessary for the flow of messages into and out of each, the clearinghouses and their directors fit this definition as they perform their important role in the diffusion of knowledge through the ERIC program.

ERIC Vocabulary Development and Control

Authorities on information retrieval systems agree that the indexing language and its structure are the primary components upon which the ultimate utility and effectiveness of the entire system depend. A great variety of techniques have been developed to analyze documents so that their contents will be relevant to the users of information systems. The terms initially used to describe the information contained in a document are taken from the document itself. These may not be the words or terms which are finally used in the information retrieval system—in fact, they may become standardized, transformed, or even coded. Whether the final form is a detailed subject-authority with definitions, scope notes, references and cross-references, or a list of permuted terms, the fact is that in many information systems vocabulary control begins with terms implicit in the records themselves. The transition from a process of "full indexing"—natural language format—to the sophisticated format of a systematic thesaurus is a logical step in applying control to the immense variety in natural language.

In the ERIC program, the *Thesaurus of ERIC Descriptors* was developed under the direction of the Panel on Educational Terminology. Using a "core" of terms, or descriptors, which had been derived from the previously mentioned indexing project on the disadvantaged, the panel manipulated that file into a thesaurus format. As the ERIC system has evolved, so has the scope and depth of the *Thesaurus,* and today only established terms taken from the *Thesaurus* may be used for indexing ERIC documents. Clearinghouses may propose new terms, but these must be accompanied by a detailed justification of their need. Each candidate term is then reviewed by a lexicographic team of subject and thesaurus specialists and is either accepted or rejected.

The decentralized nature of the ERIC system requires constant monitoring to identify areas of possible terminological overlap among the subject responsibilities of the clearinghouses. The policy of centralized lexicographic review and control provides overall balance in the system, which is not always easily accomplished at the local clearinghouse level. Two aspects of ERIC pose special lexicographic problems. First, the wide scope of the subject matter calls for a plethora of descriptors, while systems and technical considerations require counter-restraints to keep the number of descriptors from growing too large. Second, the wide range of interests and professional orientations of ERIC users force the indexer to make difficult decisions as to the apportioning of the relatively few indexing terms allotted to each document. For example, the indexer may have to choose between broad descriptors for the general educational community and highly specialized terms for the subject expert. While the desired policy is to do both, eventually technical or systems considerations may force a compromise in the final decision.

Preparation and Handling of Information

The flow of information through the ERIC system can best be described by referring to the flow chart entitled "Information Flow through *Research in Education,*" which illustrates the flow of documents from producers of information into the system and out to users (*see* fig. 1).

One major objective of the documentation aspect of the ERIC program is to ensure the comprehensive, systematic acquisition of individual reports from thousands of sources in the United States and selected English-language sources overseas. In practice, this objective is fulfilled, in large measure, by clearinghouse responsibilities to canvass the field regularly in search of unpublished and often fugitive reports or documents. This may involve the development of wide-ranging surveillance activities, such as establishing frequent contacts with state departments of education and various professional organizations, as well as monitoring conference programs and other professional meetings. Another aspect of the acquisition effort is channeled through Central ERIC, in which the staff at the central agency solicits materials for input into clearinghouses from all federal agencies and federally supported research programs. This effort includes research and development centers and regional laboratories. The National Education Association also cooperates with Central ERIC in this manner.

Document processing, or input control, is an effort to insure that reports of dubious interest or marginal quality will be discarded. In fact, each accessioned document must meet standardized requirements for photo-reproduction and copyright or reproduction privileges, as well as qualifications regarding the uniqueness and timeliness of the information. Economic considerations necessitate that only one clearinghouse process a given document for input to RIE. After acquisition and screening, each document is then cataloged according to the bibliographic requirements of the *ERIC Report Résumé* form. Entries on the résumé describe a document

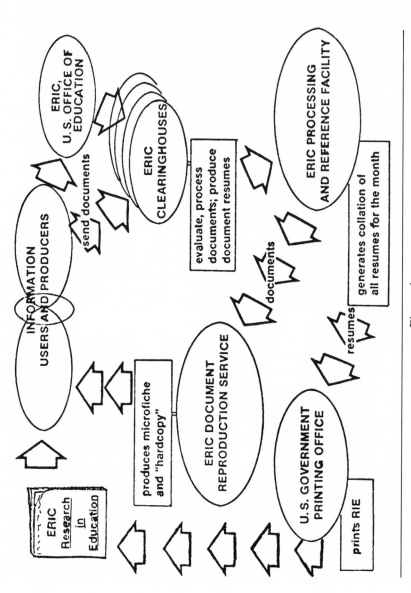

Figure 1

Information flow through *Research in Education*

in much the same manner as a main entry with added entries in the traditional library card catalog. After cataloging, the document is analyzed according to the principles of coordinate indexing, using the *Thesaurus of ERIC Descriptors* as the subject authority list. Final processing includes the development of an abstract of no more than 200 words which summarizes the contents of the document in a clear and concise manner. One copy of the original document with the completed résumé form is then forwarded to the ERIC Processing and Reference Facility.

ERIC Processing and Reference Facility

Under contract with the U.S. Office of Education, LEASCO Systems and Research Corporation currently operates the ERIC Processing and Reference Facility in Bethesda, Maryland. The ERIC facility serves as a "switching center, for it receives materials from all components of the system, records and redirects some, stores, manipulates, and reformats others, and makes the scheduled and on-demand product deliveries that keep the network functioning well."[5]

At the facility, input from the various clearinghouses is checked for the completeness of each shipment, attachment of Office of Education policy statements and reproduction releases when required, accuracy, and compliance with the procedures in the *ERIC Operating Manual*. After editing, the résumés are keyed onto paper tape, using Friden Flexowriters. When this version has been proofed against the original, the paper tape is converted to magnetic tape for further processing. High-speed digital computers are used to manipulate the files and prepare the tape versions of RIE. When all records have been verified, the computer assigns the ED accession number. The input is then merged into a weekly up-date file, which ultimately becomes a magnetic tape designed for input to the Master Typography Program of the U.S. Government Printing Office (GPO). RIE is printed by a Linotron electronic photocomposition device and marketed on a subscription basis by GPO.

From another tape, produced concurrently, each résumé announced in RIE is computer-printed in a one-page format. These single-frame résumés are matched with their respective documents by clearinghouse accession number, the ED number is added to the document, and both résumé and document are transmitted to the EDRS contractor to be microfilmed.

The ERIC facility itself serves as a clearinghouse, in that it processes completely those documents which do not fall into the scope of any clearinghouse in the ERIC network. In like manner, the facility reviews, annotates, and indexes articles in educational periodicals that do not fall into the scope of the clearinghouses and contributes this information to Macmillan Information, publisher of the *Current Index to Journals in Education*.

At various intervals specified by Central ERIC, the facility produces certain internal publications for use in the network. Among others, these include the "Thesaurus Working Copy," "Thesaurus Hierarchical Display," "Thesaurus Rotated Display," "Descriptor Usage/Statistical Report," and the "Identifier Usage/Statistical Report."

At quarterly intervals, the last three issues of RIE and CIJE are stripped from the Master Data sets, converted to a completely upper-case format, and duplicated for sale and distribution to users. Under special authorization by the Office of Education, the ERIC Facility Contractor (LEASCO Systems and Research Corporation) offers three master files for sale. The *Report Résumé* file, known as *RESUMAST,* consists of résumés of all reports which have been announced in RIE; the *Journal Article Résumé* file, with the data set designation *CIJEMAST,* includes résumés of journal articles appearing in CIJE; while *THESMAST* includes the entire *Thesaurus of ERIC Descriptors*. These master files are disseminated on magnetic tape, in either nine-track (1600 or 800 BPI) or seven-track (800 or 556 BPI) format, in the form of IBM S/360 Operating System variable length records.

ERIC Products and Services

Research in Education (RIE)

RIE, the first major product of the ERIC program, is a monthly journal announcing completed research reports, regardless of their source or point of origin, and other fugitive documents which normally would not be given wide dissemination. RIE is made up of document résumés and subject, author, and institution indexes. The résumés (abstracts) highlight the significance of each document and are listed sequentially in the Document Section by ED number (ERIC Document). The indexes, which follow the résumés, cite each document by title and ED number. For the full bibliographic citation the user must return to the Document Résumé Section. The subject, author (investigator), and institution indexes are cumulated annually in a single volume. The résumés are not cumulated and in searching this file, one must therefore proceed from the annual indexes to the monthly issues of RIE to locate specific résumés. As of 30 June 1972, RIE included 50,226 citations. Monthly input from each clearinghouse averages fifty documents.

Current Index to Journals in Education (CIJE)

CIJE was created in April 1969 as a monthly index to more than 500 journals dealing with education and education-related topics. Coverage of the journal literature is intended to be comprehensive, rather than selective, and therefore articles on education from peripheral journals not usually associated with the field are also included.

CIJE is arranged into five sections: Main Entry Section, Subject Index, Journal Contents Index, Source Journal Index, and Author Index. In the Main Entry Section, articles are classified in fifty-two descriptor groups taken from the *Thesaurus of ERIC Descriptors*. Entries describing the articles provide full bibliographic information including annotations of interpretive summaries. An EJ number (Education Journal) identifies each entry. Each article is indexed with as many as five subject headings. The Journal Contents Index lists the journals in alphabetical order, giving the date of the journal and the title of the article indexed. The Source Journal Index in each issue is a listing of the journals covered in the reference work.

CIJE is published by Macmillan Information in cooperation with Central ERIC. In addition to broad coverage, a unique characteristic of CIJE is its overall timeliness. A policy of firm scheduling between periodical publishers and ERIC clearinghouses is designed to enhance rapid processing and announcement and, when possible, clearinghouses work from proof copies or preliminary editions.

ERIC Tape Services

A number of searching and retrieval systems have been developed for use with *ERICTAPES*. In February 1970, Central ERIC announced the availability of QUERY, a software package purchased from the Computer Resources Corporation for use at approved locations such as ERIC clearinghouses, regional educational laboratories, and research and development centers. The IBM 360 model of QUERY, a proprietary search system, has been used successfully in locations such as clearinghouses and state and local educational agencies.

Search services on *ERICTAPES* are available from a number of universities, commercial organizations, federal agencies, and other institutions. For example, the Information Retrieval Department of the Lockheed Research Laboratories has announced the availability of specific subject searches of the ERIC file using the ERIC/DIALOG system. Although the system is used for on-line interactive searching, individuals who do not have direct access to the system can request a specific search of up to ten descriptors from the ERIC *Thesaurus* and up to 100 citations. Lockheed will also provide standing searches on specific subjects on a quarterly basis. In addition, the Systems Development Corporation established the SDC/ERIC search service in September 1971, which provides on-line, interactive retrieval access to the ERIC report and journal literature. The SDC/ERIC data base is linked with the TYMSHARE Corporation's nationwide communication network in thirty-two cities. The New England Research Application Center (NERAC) at the University of Connecticut is providing retrospective and selective dissemination of information (SDI) searches of the ERIC file. The search output includes the document number, title, author, citation, abstract, and index terms. There is no minimum number of searches, nor any fixed cost.

Summary

In recent years, as a concern for the transfer of information to the user has been expressed by many groups in a variety of ways, an attitude of urgency has developed, particularly on the part of those concerned with research and development activities, who have found that an effective communications system is a crucial ingredient in their work. Many automated data bases and information retrieval systems are being developed in response to this need. In this regard, the Educational Resources Information Center is presented as a model of the ways in which an information retrieval system may develop, process, and disseminate information.

Notes

1. Lorraine Mathies, "The Educational Resources Information Center; An Agent of Change," *Journal of Educational Data Processing* 7:124 (Apr. 1970).
2. *ERIC Clearinghouse Scope of Interest Manual* (Bethesda, Md.: ERIC Processing and Reference Facility, 1971), p. 34.
3. *ERIC Clearinghouse Scope of Interest Manual*, p. 7.
4. Richard S. Farr, *Knowledge Linkers and the Flow of Educational Information* (Stanford, Calif.: ERIC Clearinghouse on Educational Media and Technology, 1969), p. 1.
5. W. Ted Brandhorst, "ERIC Improving Education—That's What It's All About," *The LEASCO Magazine* 2:27 (Jan./Feb. 1971).

2

Document
Processing
in ERIC

Introduction

In the typical library context, the processing of materials encompasses all procedures necessary for the acquisition and preparation of those materials for use by patrons. These activities include the processes of selection, acquisitions, and cataloging, as well as the physical preparations of marking and binding. Variations on each of these practices occur in document processing for the ERIC system, which is illustrative of document processing procedures used in other computerized information programs. For purposes of clarity, primary attention will be given to the processing activities of ERIC clearinghouses, particularly as they are reflected in the use of the *ERIC Report Résumé* form (OE Form 6000) and the *ERIC Journal Article Résumé* form (OE Form 6027). The *Report Résumé* form (*see* fig.2) is used for processing research reports and their accompanying abstracts for publication in *Research in Education,* and the *Journal Article Résumé* form (*see* fig.3) is designated for basic input to the publishing system for the *Current Index to Journals in Education.* "Guidelines for Descriptive Cataloging," section 3.4.1, *ERIC Operating Manual,* 1971 edition,[1] was used as the principal source of information for this chapter.

Clearinghouse Responsibilities in Document Processing

The initial role of the clearinghouse in the ERIC system involves the acquisition and selection of research reports for the ERIC data base, and includes a variety of procedures and decisions. First, an intensive program for the acquisition of unpublished, fugitive research materials must be mounted to cover all aspects of individual clearinghouse subject responsibilities. Second, each document received must be evaluated with regard to its "worth," determined by its design, findings, relevance, and so on. Third, documents processed for ERIC must reflect U.S. Office of Education policy; that is, opinions and viewpoints expressed in a given document must be attributed to the originating author or organization. Fourth, the printing quality must be examined to determine whether the document can be photoreproduced to provide readable copy. Fifth, authority to reproduce copyrighted materials must be obtained from the holder of the copyright; and, sixth, procedures must be followed to ensure that only a single copy of each document will be processed for the ERIC system.

A number of specific activities must be performed in order to accomplish each of the above responsibilities. Among others, they include logging the receipt of documents, checking for duplication in the ERIC system, assigning clearinghouse accession numbers, and reporting new acquisitions to Central ERIC. The "receipts logging" procedure in an ERIC clearinghouse is actually an accounting of materials received; the information recorded about a document includes the date received, receiving individual, document title, author, source, order number (if any), quantity, condition of the item, and its disposition. Once an item has been acquired and logged, a check is made to determine previous processing or accession for processing by another clearinghouse. This can be determined in part from the monthly Clearinghouse Acquisitions Data List, an inventory of all newly accessioned documents in the system displayed in alphabetical order by author and title. This list is compiled by the ERIC Facility Contractor from ERIC Clearinghouse Acquisitions Data forms which are sent to the facility on the last working day of each month. Variations in the manner of creating author citations necessitate close checking for possible duplication. The ERIC Clearinghouse Acquisitions Data List is only one of the references used for duplicate checking. All candidate documents must also be matched against prior ERIC document listings, as well as all issues of RIE and any other published lists of ERIC documents.

Descriptive Cataloging

Descriptive cataloging in the ERIC system is the process which describes the physical appearance of documents, tags them for ultimate retrieval, and produces information for the various indexes to the ERIC data base. The basic difference between traditional cataloging, done on 3" x 5" library cards, and cataloging for ERIC and other information retrieval systems is that the catalog records needed for the ERIC program are assembled on a *Report Résumé* form (known in other information systems as a "data sheet" or an "input sheet") for further manipulation by the computer. In other words, although a completed *Report Résumé* form represents a traditional 3" x 5" catalog card, in document processing for the ERIC system, that information will not appear in the same arrangement again. Therefore, the cataloger in a clearinghouse must consider each entry on the résumé form as a distinct entity, one which most accurately tags a document on the basis of the information given. Listings on the résumé form describe a document in much the same manner as the main entry for a book with added entries in a library's card catalog. Standards for descriptive cataloging in ERIC are derived from the *COSATI Standard for Descriptive Cataloging of Government Scientific and Technical Reports*[2] and the *Anglo-American Cataloging Rules.*[3]

ERIC Report Résumé (Figure 2)

The guidelines for processing documents presented here are a summary of instructions which have been developed for use by ERIC clearinghouses. They are structured in reference to the appropriate field of the *Report Résumé,* the basic input to this information system. These notes are in no way intended to provide detailed directions on processing problems; instead they are presented as an overview of the similarities and differences in ways of preparing information for storage and retrieval.

The *Report Résumé* form is used to identify bibliographic data and other information about each document acquired, processed, and stored within the ERIC system. Certain elements of data in fields of the *Report Résumé* are of fixed length, as, for example, the Clearinghouse Accession Number and the Program Area Code (P.A.). However, most fields are of variable length, as is the case with the title of the document and the abstract. The maximum span of any variable-length field is determined by the amount of space available on the *Report Résumé* form, which has been designed for pica type (ten characters per inch), although a typewriter with elite type (twelve characters per inch) can be used. The only limitation imposed on the length of individual lines typed in any of the variable-length fields is the width of the form. As many characters as possible per line is acceptable. However, *hyphenation is not permitted at the end of a line.* Failure to follow this rule will create the necessity of an editorial change at Central ERIC prior to paper tape preparation. The reason for this rule is that when the computer reads a line of characters to format data into an array for processing, it is programmed to determine the end of a word by

OE FORM 6000, 2/69				DEPARTMENT OF HEALTH, EDUCATION, AND WELFARE OFFICE OF EDUCATION	
ERIC ACC. NO.				ERIC REPORT RESUME	

CH ACC. NO.	P.A.	PUBL. DATE	ISSUE	IS DOCUMENT COPYRIGHTED?	YES ☐ NO ☐
				ERIC REPRODUCTION RELEASE?	YES ☐ NO ☐
				LEVEL OF AVAILABILITY	I☐ II☐ III☐

AUTHOR

TITLE

SOURCE CODE | INSTITUTION (SOURCE)

SP. AG. CODE | SPONSORING AGENCY

EDRS PRICE | CONTRACT NO. | GRANT NO.

REPORT NO. | BUREAU NO.

AVAILABILITY

JOURNAL CITATION

DESCRIPTIVE NOTE

DESCRIPTORS

IDENTIFIERS

ABSTRACT

GPO 870-390

Figure 2
ERIC Report Résumé

finding the space occurring after the last character in a word. It automatically adds one space after the last word in a line. Thus, if "re-" were
typed at the end of one line and "trieve" began the next, the computer
would read this as two distinct words, and the final copy would appear as
"re- trieve."

Upper and lower case letters are used in the author, title, institution,
sponsoring agency, availability, journal citation, descriptive note, descriptor, identifier, and abstract fields. The semicolon is used as a delimiter, a
character which serves as a method of dividing certain fields into subfields. Major use of the semicolon as a delimiter is made to separate
authors, source codes, contract numbers, descriptors, identifiers, and the
like. The semicolon does not function as a delimiter in the title and
abstract fields, and it may be used in those fields in the normal manner.

Specifications regarding the use of special print characters and other
details concerning the manipulation of the *ERIC Report Résumé* as required for inputting materials are *not* presented here. Instead, an explanation of the components of the résumé is given.

1. *ERIC Accession Number* (ED Prefix). The ERIC accession number
is assigned by the computer to each résumé and its corresponding document
prior to final processing into the ERIC system by the ERIC Facility Contractor. This accession number consists of a two-letter alphabetic prefix
ED (for ERIC Document) followed by six numerics, such as ED 034 928.

The ERIC accession number satisfies several requirements. It serves as
an address tag for storing and locating individual documents, an address for
use in the announcement media, and an order number for acquiring microfiche or hard copy from the ERIC Document Reproduction Service.

2. *Clearinghouse Accession Number.* Each ERIC clearinghouse has
been given a two-letter alphabetic prefix for use in assigning accession
numbers to documents processed into their individual collections. The
following are examples of alphabetic prefixes which were generated primarily from the subject area designations of the clearinghouses:

Subject Coverage of Clearinghouses	Alphabetic Prefixes
Exceptional Children	EC
Higher Education	HE
Library and Information Science	LI
Social Science/Social Studies	SO
Vocational and Technical Education	VT

The clearinghouse accession number then consists of the two-letter alphabetic prefix followed by six numerics, such as LI 062 091. Once it has
been assigned, the accession number provides a convenient way of relating

document surrogates, completed résumés, and other forms to the original document.

3. *P.A.* (Program Area). Interim and final reports for projects (contracts or grants) funded by the National Center for Research and Educational Development of the U.S. Office of Education are a part of the input to the ERIC system. The Program Area code identifies the legislative authority under which the project was funded; thus Code 24 stands for Cooperative Research, PL 89–10, Title IV. This code must be entered on the *Report Résumé* form as two characters. Example:

```
┌─────────────┐
│ P.A.        │
│             │
│ 24          │
│             │
└─────────────┘
```

4. *Publication Date.* If the date of publication is unknown, the year of the copyright date or the date on which the work was completed may be used. The publication date is entered by day, month, and year in the following manner:

```
┌─────────────┐
│ Publ. Date  │
│             │
│ 22May72     │
│             │
└─────────────┘
```

5. *Issue.* The purpose of this field is to assign a *Report Résumé* to the issue of *Research in Education* in which it will appear. The issue designation is determined by the ERIC Facility Contractor and entered on the *Report Résumé* form prior to the preparation of the paper tape.

6. *Copyright Information; ERIC Reproduction Release; Level of Availability.* It is the responsibility of the cataloger to determine whether the document being processed is copyrighted, and to report that fact to the ERIC system. This is done by ticking the "yes" or "no" box in response to the question, "Is document copyrighted?" on the *Report Résumé* form. If the document or any part of it is copyrighted, then the clearinghouse must obtain a reproduction release from the holder of the copyright before any processing can occur. The clearinghouse is responsible for maintaining a file of reproduction releases and for ensuring the accuracy of information checked on the *Report Résumé* form.

Three categories, known as "level of availability," have been developed to symbolize the availability of a report in the ERIC system. An "X," designating the level, is entered in the appropriate box at the upper right of the *Report Résumé* form.

Level I Documents. A copyrighted document for which a reproduction release has been obtained, or a report which has not been copyrighted, is classified as a Level I document. In effect, this means that both microfiche and hardcopies of such reports are available through the ERIC Document Reproduction Service.

Level II Documents. A copyright holder may grant permission to reproduce a document in microfiche only. This type of reproduction release is classified as Level II. Noncopyrighted materials may also be classified as Level II. If so, the availability of hardcopy is entered in the Availability Field on the *Report Résumé* form. Government Printing Office publications that are for sale from the Superintendent of Documents, as well as sale items from the National Education Association, are processed at Levels II or III.

Level III Documents. Copyrighted documents which are not released for reproduction are classified as Level III. This means that neither microfiche nor hardcopy is available through the ERIC Document Reproduction Service. An excellent example of this type of restriction is illustrated in the control over reproductions of doctoral dissertations held by University Microfilms. Dissertations may be, and are, indexed and abstracted for *Research in Education.* However, all reproduction rights are retained by University Microfilms, and copies may only be obtained from that source. In all instances where microfiche and/or hardcopy are not available through the ERIC Document Reproduction Service, an alternate source for obtaining the report should be entered in the Availability Field. The information entered there should be as complete as possible so that a user of RIE may order a copy of the document. It should include the full name and address of the source, as well as the price of the report.

7. *Author.* Personal authors, compilers and editors of documents, or the principal investigator of a research project are indicated in this field. The names are entered in full (last name first) as given on the document, omitting titles, degrees, and other honorifics.

8. *Title.* The Title Field contains the complete title of a document, including any alternative title or subtitle, or other relevant associated descriptive matter. A series title should follow the specific title of the document. A semicolon is generally used to separate a title from a subtitle or other alternative information. Titles of conference proceedings and the like should be taken verbatim from the title page. The number, place, and date of the conference should be placed in parentheses after the title and followed by a period.

9. *Source Code and Institution* (Source). The institution (source) is the corporate author or organizational source of a document. Governments

and their agencies, societies, institutions, universities, firms, and conferences, which are clearly indicated as incorporated, are to be regarded as the sources responsible for the documents. The *ERIC Source Directory* is an alphabetical listing of all institutional sources used in the ERIC system, with their respective source codes. The individual source code listing is entered in this field, as:

> Source Code
> JXQ12600

Institutions for which no code exists in the *ERIC Source Directory* should be entered by the clearinghouse by name in the Institution (Source) Field. The entry should conform to the COSATI *Standard* and should be as complete as possible. Source codes will then be added to the *Report Résumé* form during the editing process at the ERIC facility.

10. *Sponsoring Agency and Sp. Ag. Code.* Reports of research performed under contracts or grants from a government agency, such as the National Center for Educational Research and Development, or from private foundations, are entered under the sponsoring agency. The code for the agency is entered in that field. A source code will be assigned later during the ending process at the ERIC facility, and will be added to the next update of the *Source Directory*.

11. *EDRS Price.* The Educational Documents Reproduction Service is the agency responsible for the sale of documents indexed in RIE. The EDRS price for microfiche or hardcopy of a document is based upon the number of pages that must be photographed. Pagination is based on the total number of printed pages including diagrams, charts, illustrations, maps, and the like, whether numbered or not. The clearinghouse is responsible for reporting the page count according to the EDRS pricing schedule for Level I and Level II documents. Present pricing procedures are calculated from a basic unit price for microfiche, and an increment of 100 pages for hardcopy. Document costs are included in the tape edition of RIE.

12. *Contract Number.* The contract number is the numeric identifier which designates the financial support for the work or research reported in the document; thus, OEC–4–6–0608230–634 indicates a contract supported by the U.S. Office of Education.

13. *Grant Number.* In the same manner as above, the grant number is the numeric identifier which designates the financial support for the work or research reported in the document; thus, OEG–4–6–000516–0962 indicates a U.S. Office of Education grant.

14. *Report Number.* The report number may be the unique alpha-numeric identification assigned to the report by the corporate author or originating agency, or it may be the unique number assigned to the re-port by an agency other than the originating agency. Many report numbers consist of letters representing the originating or monitoring agency fol-lowed by a unique number, such as CCHE–1019. Often report numbers include descriptive words such as "bulletin" or "research paper." These may be ignored or abbreviated with no punctuation as follows: Bull or RP.

15. *USOE Project Control Number.* All Office of Education contractor reports entered into the ERIC system must have a Project Control number such as BR–6–8319. At present the National Center for Educational Re-search and Development, formerly the USOE Bureau of Research, utilizes a Project Control Number beginning with the prefix "BR" as in the example.

16. *Availability.* When microfiche and/or hardcopy of a document is not available from the ERIC Document Reproduction Service (Levels II and III), an alternative source for obtaining the document should be identified in this field. That information will appear after the citation of the document in RIE.

17. *Journal Citation.* This field presents the journal citations for ar-ticles from periodicals entered into *Research In Education*. The informa-tion optimally includes the journal title, volume number, issue number, pagination, and the date. The journal name is always followed by a semi-colon.

18. *Descriptive Note.* Two distinct types of information are entered in this field: the pagination of the document, as determined previously for the EDRS price, and descriptive information concerning preprints, re-prints, papers or speeches presented at annual conferences, and so on. If the document represents a speech or a published paper, the descriptive note should include a bibliographic reference to the source of the item, whether a preprint or a published paper. Pagination is always the first item entered in this field.

19. *Descriptors.* Descriptors are the terms found in the *Thesaurus of ERIC Descriptors* which are selected to describe the contents of ERIC documents. Descriptors are classified as either major or minor. Major descriptors are those terms which indicate the major subject of the docu-ment, and are entered in the Descriptor Field preceded by an asterisk. The asterisk serves as an indicator to the computer program that the descriptor should appear in the subject index of *Research in Education* and it also alerts the user of RIE browsing through the résumé section. A maximum number of five major terms may be assigned to each document. Minor descriptors further index the document and may be used in a computer search of RIE.

20. *Identifiers.* Certain categories of terms, such as acronyms, projects,

test names, trade names, and the like often receive extensive coverage in ERIC documents. Although by their nature such terms cannot be structured into the vocabulary of ERIC descriptors, the extent of their use frequently justifies document retrieval. As with descriptors, major identifiers should be preceded by asterisks so that they will print in *Research in Education;* no more than one major identifier can be assigned per résumé. Any major identifier must not exceed fifty spaces in the identifier field, for this is all that the indexes will print in RIE. The logical removal of prepositions, articles, and conjunctions to bring the identifier within the space limitations is permitted.

21. *Abstract.* The ERIC abstract provides information to assist the users of the system looking for material relevant to their needs. The system calls for either of two types of abstracts: the INFORMATIVE, which *summarizes* the contents of a document by condensing its major ideas, and the INDICATIVE, which *describes* the contents of a document and what it is about. In preparing an INFORMATIVE abstract, the abstractor writes as if he were the author, presenting an objective summary of his ideas with a maximum amount of information. By contrast, in an INDICATIVE abstract, the abstractor writes from the point of view of an informed but impartial reader, describing the contents and format of a document. An INFORMATIVE abstract contains a statement of the author's thesis, several sentences of his development or proof, and his conclusions. An INDICATIVE abstract broadly reports what is discussed or included in the document, in what manner the information is presented, and, if necessary, to whom the document is addressed. In short, the INFORMATIVE abstract is a condensed duplication of a document's contents, while an INDICATIVE abstract is a guide to its contents.

Brevity and clarity are essential characteristics of a well-written abstract. The minimum requirement of each abstract in the ERIC program is a statement of the subject and scope of the document in (usually) no more than 200 words. The abstractor's initials are entered at the end of the abstract and enclosed in parentheses.

ERIC Journal Article Résumé (Figure 3)

The *Current Index to Journals in Education* is a monthly bulletin designed to provide bibliographic access to the journal literature in education and related fields. Many characteristics of CIJE processing are identical to those required for preparing report literature for *Research in Education.* Processing instructions will be referred to only when appropriate, rather than duplicated in their entirety.

Periodicals selected for CIJE processing fall into two categories: (1) journals of education and other fields, wholly or primarily within the scope

ERIC JOURNAL ARTICLE RESUME

ERIC ACC. NO.		
CH. ACC. NO.	GROUP CODE	

AUTHOR

TITLE

JOURNAL CITATION

DESCRIPTORS

IDENTIFIERS

ANNOTATION

EDIT NOTES

OE FORM 6027, 10/69   REPLACES OE FORM 6027, 4/69, WHICH IS OBSOLETE.

Figure 3
ERIC Journal Article Résumé

of a single ERIC clearinghouse (core journals); (2) education and other journals not primarily within the scope of a single clearinghouse, journals relevant to two or more clearinghouses, and those outside the scope of any clearinghouse.

Periodicals in the first category are assigned for processing by Central ERIC to one of the individual clearinghouses. Those in the second group are processed at the ERIC facility. Qualitative selection is not applied in choosing journal articles, since the nature of the CIJE program is to be comprehensive, rather than selective. Coverage of articles in the core education journals is "cover-to-cover" for each issue which, in this instance, is defined as complete article coverage for a given journal, ignoring such items as book reviews, feature columns, editorials, letters to the editor, and the like. Articles in *noncore journals* are selected for inclusion in CIJE strictly on the basis of their relationship to the field of education.

Quick announcement of the journal literature is the goal of CIJE. A journal article is entered into CIJE based upon the date when it is received for processing, *not* the date of issue by the publisher. Often there is a serious lag between the time a journal is published and the time it is actually delivered to its subscribers. Therefore, strong efforts are made to obtain proof copies or preliminary editions, so as to expedite the CIJE announcement of articles.

The data sheet used for basic input to the CIJE publishing system is the *ERIC Journal Article Résumé* form (*see* fig.3). Bibliographic data for each article processed within the system are identified through its use. Three fields (elements of data) are of fixed length. These are the CIJE and Clearinghouse Accession Numbers and the Group Code. The other fields are of variable length; their maximum length is determined by the amount of space available on the form and is limited only by the width of the form blocks. Hyphenation is never permitted at the end of lines. The procedures of descriptive cataloging and indexing used for CIJE are typical of those required for input to *Research in Education,* since the *ERIC Journal Article Résumé* form is merely a simple, modified version of that used for the report literature. Only specific differences relevant to journal article résumés and specifications unique to the processing of periodical literature are discussed.

1. *CIJE Accession Number* (EJ Prefix). Each journal article résumé in the CIJE publishing system receives a unique accession number with an EJ prefix, which identifies the résumé by providing an address tag for announcement, storage, and retrieval. It consists of the two-letter alphabetic prefix EJ (for ERIC Journal), followed by six numerics; for example, EJ 032 123. The accession number is assigned just prior to publication.

2. *Clearinghouse Accession Number.* In assigning accession numbers to journal articles, each clearinghouse and the ERIC facility use the same two-letter alphabetic prefix. That alpha prefix is followed by six numerics, such as AC 500 123, LI 500 791, and TE 200 932. A unique series of numerics, the 500 000 series (or in the case of the Clearinghouse on the Teaching of English, the 200 000 and the 700 000 series) has been set aside to be used solely for identifying journal article résumés. A résumé assigned an accession number in this series is immediately associated with CIJE.

3. *Descriptor Group Code.* A three-digit number is entered for each journal article résumé to identify the major subject grouping of its content. Such grouping provides a vertical subject file for the printed résumé section of the CIJE publication, and is assigned in addition to the usual subject indexing. Descriptor Groups identified by these codes are mutually exclusive, and only *one* code is assigned to any given résumé. The Descriptor Groups, with their respective three-digit group code numbers and scope notes, are found in the *Thesaurus of ERIC Descriptors.* An example of a code name and number with a scope note follows:

330 Library Science
   The principles and practices related
   to processing conducted in the library
   as well as related user requirements
   and services, e.g., Abstracting,
   Information Dissemination, Library
   Services, etc.

4. *Personal Author(s).* The author is the name of the person(s) who wrote the article being processed and/or performed the work described in the article. Author entries should be in upper and lower case.

5. *Title.* This field contains the complete title of the article being processed with alternative or subtitles. Entries must be in upper and lower case.

6. *Journal Citation.* Information about the journal citation must include the journal title, volume number, issue number (if available), pagination, and date. The journal title is *always* followed by a semicolon (a delimiter, as in the author field); this facilitates production of an index of journal titles. All journal titles are entered in a full unabbreviated form with the exception of initial articles, which are dropped.

7. *Descriptors.* Descriptors are terms taken from the *Thesaurus of ERIC Descriptors* used to index the subject matter of the articles announced in CIJE. As with the report literature, descriptors are classified as major and minor terms. A major descriptor must be preceded by an asterisk when it is entered in the Descriptor field; this signals the computer

program to place that descriptor in the subject index of CIJE. No more than five major descriptors, nor more than a total of ten descriptors including identifiers, may be used per résumé. Most articles should require no more than three major subject indexing points.

8. *Identifiers.* As with report literature, identifiers are terms which provide subject indexing in addition to descriptors. They are neither cross-referenced nor structured and, therefore, do not appear in the vocabulary of the *Thesaurus of ERIC Descriptors.* Identifiers are entered in upper and lower case with the exception of acronyms, which are all upper case. The maximum length of an identifier for printing in the subject index is fifty characters, including spaces.

Identifiers are classed as major or minor, and no more than one major identifier can be assigned to each résumé. A major identifier must be preceded by an asterisk when entered in its field and, as with report literature, it will appear in the subject index of CIJE. Minor identifiers will appear only in the résumé section of the publication. No more than a total of ten subject indexing points, nor more than five asterisked points (including both descriptors and identifiers), are used per résumé.

9. *Annotation.* If the scope and value of an article are not adequately expressed in the bibliographic citation, an annotation of no more than fifty words may be included in CIJE on a selective basis. Unlike abstracts for *Research in Education,* the annotation may include a *positive evaluation* of an article, the author's point of view or major bias, as well as a statement concerning the type and scope of the report or study, the intended audience, qualifications of the author, and any special features. The annotation should readily alert the user to material pertinent to his interests. It should be included in one paragraph and not duplicate information already provided in the title or descriptors.

10. *Edit Notes.* Clearinghouses leave this space blank. It is reserved for editorial comment from the publisher of CIJE.

Summary

The development of machine-readable, bibliographic data bases is dependent upon processing procedures already familiar to many librarians and other information specialists. The ERIC system serves as an effective model of the in-house preparation of documents for an automated file.

Notes

1. "Guidelines for Descriptive Cataloging," *ERIC Operating Manual* (Bethesda, Md.: ERIC Processing and Reference Facility, LEASCO Systems and Research Corp., 1971), Section 3.4.1.

2. *COSATI Standard for Descriptive Cataloging of Government Scientific and Technical Reports* (Springfield, Va.: National Technical Information Service, 1966).
3. *Anglo-American Cataloging Rules* (Chicago: American Library Assn., 1967).

3

Vocabulary Development and Control*

Introduction

Information systems, whether in the traditional format of libraries or in the more specialized concept of subject-oriented information centers, are, for all practical purposes, dependent upon the fact that their resources must be described by the terms found in standardized, authoritative, subject vocabularies. The problems related to the creation or discovery of such vocabularies are fundamental to the development and use of information resources. In a multidisciplinary field such as education, the complications are extensive, since many basic education concepts are best expressed by phrases and sentences—or even paragraphs—rather than single or compound word forms, as in the sciences. In addition, much of the terminology in education occurs in everyday usage and is often of temporary duration, eventually becoming adapted for specialized application. Words like *coordination* (of muscles or of programs), *articulation* (of speech or of programs), or *adjustment* (of equipment or personality) are examples of

* Information regarding vocabulary control in the ERIC program was derived from the "Thesaurus of ERIC Descriptors Guidelines," Section 3.4.4, of the 1971 edition of the *ERIC Operating Manual.*

common terms with multiple meanings. This is a particularly serious problem for users of the research literature in education, especially in its experimental aspects, where users require clear, concise identification of the elements of an experiment and the relationships between them as for example, the methodology of a study in relation to its findings. Furthermore, the specific language requirements of an indexing system as opposed to (or in conjunction with) the requisites for successful and continuing search programs are, in many cases, as yet unknown. In fact, the storage of knowledge in automated files has stimulated a new look at the whole concept and practice of indexing.

Machine-readable bibliographic data bases, such as the ERIC files, MEDLARS, and MARC tapes, constitute a new approach to information handling. Since, like all works of reference, they exist primarily to show users where the complete information may be found, they must provide accurate and significant access to the literature which they represent, whether by author, title, subject, abstract, or, as is customary, a combination of these. The ERIC system, with its principal reference tools, *Research in Education* and *Current Index to Journals in Education,* presents both a manual and a machine (computer) approach to information, each of which is contingent upon subject access through the *Thesaurus of ERIC Descriptors.* The MEDLARS program (*MEDical Literature Analysis and Retrieval System*) is a computer-based system designed to achieve rapid bibliographic access to biomedical journal information. In addition to other elements in this process, it uses *Medical Subject Headings* (MeSH), the authority list of technical terms used for indexing journal articles and cataloging books. As can be seen from the *Survey of Scientific-Technical Tape Services,* this is the prevailing pattern in computerized bibliographic information services.[1] Very few of these services allow or can operate with an uncontrolled vocabulary in the production of their data bases.

Subject Classification and Thesauri

The card catalog is traditionally regarded as the index designed to make the library's resources available to its patrons. The catalog offers such detailed bibliographic information as author, title, publisher, and the like, but only dubious access by subject. In fact, subject cataloging in large academic libraries is usually based on the *Library of Congress Subject Headings*[2] and in certain smaller library situations on *Sears List of Subject Headings.*[3] This conventional approach to classifying and organizing information usually follows two principles:

Subject classification which attempts to arrange information into patterns in such a way that we can recognize areas relevant to particular subject interests. . . . *Subject specification* which attempts to designate information in such a way that designation by [the] searcher is the same as that by [the] indexer so that a match can be made by locating items with that designation without regard to the order in which the file is stored and in particular without regard to order based on classification.[4]

However else such principles may affect large operating situations, it is obvious that there are long delays in updating classification schedules for special subject fields. This, as many librarians and information specialists know, is particularly true for the burgeoning literature of education.

Standard subject terminology lists, arranged in alphabetical order, came into use near the end of the nineteenth century. Since that time numerous subject heading lists have appeared, particularly in scientific literature. In recent years, however, a new type of alphabetical listing of authoritative indexing terms, designed primarily for information storage and retrieval systems, has been developed in the format of a thesaurus. The thesaurus best known in the English-speaking world is that of Peter Mark Roget, who published the first collection of synonyms, antonyms, and other related words in 1852. Dozens of revisions and editions have been produced from this original work, intended as a classified arrangement of words according to the ideas they express; it listed against a given term or phrase those terms or phrases synonymous or nearly synonymous with it. In other words, *Roget's Thesaurus* is a list of alternatives to be used at will. On the other hand, John R. Sharp, writing on the fundamentals of information retrieval, states that "a thesaurus . . . groups terms, not for the purpose of providing acceptable alternatives, but for the specific purpose of prohibiting the use of alternatives, there being a standard term which is to be used whenever it or any of the terms in the group arises, either in indexing or searching."[5] The *Chemical Engineering Thesaurus,* produced by the American Institute of Chemical Engineers, exemplifies the first type, while the *Thesaurus of ERIC Descriptors* typifies the latter.

Occasionally ERIC documents are also described by another set of terms not appearing in the *Thesaurus of ERIC Descriptors.* This is a familiar feature of indexing schemes such as that used in the ERIC information system; the additional group of terms is known as "identifiers." Identifiers are used for very specific phenomena, such as brand names. Unlike descriptors, they are not subject to lexicographic analysis and are not structured or cross-referenced in any way. Their major purpose is to provide terms of a specialized nature which may be used in addition to the descriptors in the *Thesaurus.* Identifiers are described in detail in chapter 4.

The information retrieval thesaurus differs from the standard word list in a variety of ways, but particularly in that it lists against a given term or phrase those terms or phrases which are synonymous or nearly synonymous with it. Other terms listed under a descriptor occur most consistently in the following order of relationships. The ERIC approach is typical:

UF	Used For
NT	Narrower Term
BT	Broader Term
RT	Related Term

Thus we see that a thesaurus establishes generic and hierarchical relationships between terms.

Example: **HYDROCARBON**
    BT   Air Pollution

AIR POLLUTION
    NT   Hydrocarbon

   or

Example: **INFORMATION RETRIEVAL**
    BT   Information Utilization

INFORMATION UTILIZATION
    NT   Information Retrieval

In other cases, where terms do not have generic relationships, but where it would be helpful to guide the indexer and user from one to another, they are linked as follows:

Example: **COOLANTS**
    RT   Brines
          Dry Ice
          Refrigerants

   or

Example: **INFORMATION PROCESSING**
    RT   Cataloging
          Feedback
          Programming Languages

Also, by using numerous cross references, the thesaurus provides many more access points for literature searching:

Example: **CATALOGING**
    UF   Bibliographic Control

   or

Example: **BIBLIOGRAPHIC CONTROL**
    USE   CATALOGING

Therefore, the thesaurus serves two primary purposes: first, to provide a basic authority list of terms which facilitate a consistent description of documents, and second, to provide a structured display of relationships between index terms as an aid in indexing and searching. Barhydt and Schmidt indicate that "in such an array, index terms are usually arranged in groups . . . each of which is then divided into smaller subgroups representing categories of words. Problems of synonyms, homonyms, and ambiguities are handled . . . by means of scope notes and cross-references of various kinds."[6] For information retrieval purposes, the thesaurus in the ERIC program is defined as follows:

> A term-associated list structured to enable indexers and subject analysts to describe the subject information of a document to a desired level of specificity at input, and to permit searchers to describe in mutually precise terms the information required at output. A thesaurus therefore serves as an authority list and as a device to bring into coincidence the language of the documents and the language of the questions.[7]

In simplest terms, therefore, a thesaurus provides the means of communication which is essential to the successful operation of an information system.

Thesaurus of ERIC Descriptors: A Model in Vocabulary Development and Control[8]

Development of the ERIC Thesaurus

The U.S. Office of Education's commitment to the establishment and operation of a national information retrieval system for the field of education carried with it an obligation to provide some form of vocabulary control. In September 1965 an advisory group called the Panel on Educational Terminology (PET) was formed to consult with the ERIC staff on the development of a thesaurus of educational terminology. In its early meetings, the panel, made up of educators and information experts, assembled observers from various subject areas in the education community. The observer group, in conjunction with panel members, provided a logical means for identifying specialized needs in the literature of education. As a result, guidelines were prepared for the "free indexing" of documents until such time as an authoritative reference source for in-depth subject analysis was available. This is, in fact, how most such specialized vocabularies originate.

Concurrent with the formation of the Panel on Educational Terminology, the "free indexing" of a collection of 1,740 documents relating to the education of disadvantaged children was completed at the Information Retrieval Center on the Disadvantaged at Yeshiva University. This project generated a terminology base of some 2,300 terms related to a broad cross-section of education. This base was used to create a more formalized thesaurus format which was in turn submitted to a selected group of educators, librarians, and information specialists for evaluation. Consequently numerous changes were made in word form and cross-reference structure in the *Thesaurus* base.

Many of the initial considerations concerning a thesaurus of educational terminology had been completed by the time that the ERIC system was first being developed. Work at the Center for Documentation and Communication Research at Case Western Reserve University in 1961 provided the prerequisites for the construction of such a thesaurus through an analysis of document and question languages, as well as a survey of the types and forms of information which users need. By 1965, actual development of an education thesaurus was underway. The product was a thesaurus of education terminology using the technique of "facet analysis" for vocabulary control.[9]

It is important to note that problems of terminology control in the ERIC system had to be solved with due regard for other dimensions of the system. The decision to establish a subject-oriented, decentralized network of information centers, coordinated by a central agency, was followed by the selection of coordinate indexing as the processing device. These principles meant that the terminology in the *Thesaurus* had to come directly from the educational literature, rather than from an independently derived authority or subject heading list.

After studying other efforts in thesaurus development, such as the rules and conventions produced by the Engineers Joint Council and Project Lex of the Office of Naval Research, the panel decided that, although these principles were not appropriate for the field of education, they were highly useful as guidelines. Therefore, in October of 1966, the panel issued a document entitled *Rules for Thesaurus Preparation;* this document, revised in 1969, includes guidelines for expanding and modifying the *Thesaurus of ERIC Descriptors* and for developing subject indexing outside the scope of the *Thesaurus,* particularly in the form of identifiers.

With the basic format of the *Thesaurus,* and the procedures to control its development, already produced, the panel formulated as additional resources in the *Thesaurus* a related series of indexes to the main body of descriptors. These comprise a Rotated Descriptor Display (essentially a Keyword-in-Context index); a synopsis of the Descriptor Groups; and a Descriptor Group Display showing every term appearing in each of the

Descriptor Groups. The Descriptor Groups, arranged in order of the three-digit group code, include a scope note, with cross-references to related descriptor groups given in most scope notes.

> *Example:* **320   Library Materials**
> Includes library collections such as Books, Annotated Bibliographies, Historical Reviews, etc. See *also* AUDIOVISUAL MATERIALS AND METHODS, COMMUNICATION.

or

> *Example:* **330   Library Science**
> The principles and practices related to processing conducted in the library as well as related user requirements and services, e.g., Abstracting, Information Dissemination, Library Services, etc.

The group code and the main group headings, for example, 330 Library Science, are also used to arrange the main entry sections of the *Current Index to Journals in Education,* so that users may focus their attention on the references in a particular subject area.

The Descriptor Group Display (*see* fig. 4) is presented so that the user may browse clusters of conceptually related terms to determine descriptor relationships and usage. This opportunity is particularly important in the structuring of new descriptors.

Search for Authority in Vocabulary Development and Control

As a model of formalized indexing and searching language, the *Thesaurus of ERIC Descriptors* is the product of numerous types of expertise and much negotiation. Frederick Goodman, Professor of Education, University of Michigan, has served as a member of the Panel on Educational Terminology since its inception in 1965. His concern is that of an academician seeking to bring vocabulary control to his own subject area. In an article entitled "The Role and Function of the Thesaurus in Education," Dr. Goodman gives a succinct presentation of the need for authority in the development and control of the vocabulary of a "soft" discipline. A portion of Dr. Goodman's article is reproduced here:

A great many terms are necessary to describe the many aspects of education, and the task of relating them in even an approximately consistent way is an enormous one. The undertaking obviously should be managed by

```
330   Library Science
      ABSTRACTING
      BIBLIOGRAPHIC COUPLING
      CATALOGING
      CLASSIFICATION
      CODIFICATION
      DATA BASES
      DECENTRALIZED LIBRARY SYSTEMS
      DOCUMENTATION
      FILING
      INDEXING
      INFORMATION DISSEMINATION
      INFORMATION NEEDS
      INFORMATION RETRIEVAL
      INFORMATION SCIENCE
      INFORMATION SERVICES
      INFORMATION STORAGE
      INFORMATION SYSTEMS
      INFORMATION UTILIZATION
      INTERLIBRARY LOANS
      LIBRARY ACQUISITION
      LIBRARY AUTOMATION
      LIBRARY CIRCULATION
      LIBRARY EXTENSION
      LIBRARY MATERIAL SELECTION
      LIBRARY NETWORKS
      LIBRARY PROGRAMS
      LIBRARY REFERENCE SERVICES
      LIBRARY SCIENCE
      LIBRARY SERVICES
      LIBRARY SURVEYS
      LIBRARY TECHNICAL PROCESSES
      MANAGEMENT INFORMATION SYSTEMS
      ON LINE SYSTEMS
      SEARCH STRATEGIES
      SUBJECT INDEX TERMS
```

Figure 4
Descriptor group display

people who not only know what they are talking about but who also should be able to predict what [those] in their field are likely to be saying in the near future. It should also enlist people who are willing to pay a great deal of attention to the details of relating one term to another within the system. To engage a large number of these two kinds of people over a long period of time is very likely to cost a great deal of money. There is little proprietary value in producing such a list of terms, for it can easily be copied, adapted, updated, etc. Thus, because of its high cost and low proprietary value, this becomes a task likely to be funded only by a government.

. . . After the decision has been made to spend money to produce an authority list, one must decide how this authority is to be delegated. The history of the development of the ERIC *Thesaurus* is an example of how this was done. Had the authority been delegated in a way which powerful segments of the educational community had not approved, money could not have bought an accepted "authority list." . . .

Prior to the indexing of the first document selected for entry into the system, there was no *Thesaurus*. When confronted with the first document, the indexer identified the concepts which he felt to be important for purposes of describing (and thus retrieving) it. Each concept was then represented by a term of the indexer's choosing. The term, formally called a "descriptor," was to reflect the language normally used in related literature to describe the concept encountered. The descriptors, fabricated for purposes of describing the first documents to go into the system, became the initial entries in the *Thesaurus*. Obviously, this procedure means that the *Thesaurus* grows as the system grows; each new document entering the system brings with it the potential for at least one new descriptor. Naturally, the indexer is expected to use any descriptors already in the *Thesaurus* rather than add new descriptors which would duplicate existing ones. It is precisely in this sense that the system controls terminology. Differences of opinion on such matters must be negotiated by clearinghouse-based indexers and ERIC Central-employed lexicographers. To the extent that ERIC Central wins out in arguments of this kind the "authority" of the system lies in ERIC Central. To the extent that clearinghouses win the arguments, the system's "authority" is decentralized. The growth of the *Thesaurus* is controlled by a constant tug-of-war between the centralizing and decentralizing tendencies built into the system.

But the process is actually more complex than this characterization implies. Most of the detailed ERIC Central lexicographic work has been done on a contract basis by private industry. North American Rockwell was the first large scale contractor. The present contract is with Leasco Systems and Research Corporation. The principle of involving private enterprise in the operation of the ERIC system appears in several other major ways. Distribution of documents, either in microfiche or hard copy form has been done by both Bell and Howell and by National Cash Register. The CCM Information Corporation, a subsidiary of Crowell Collier and Macmillan [now Macmillan Information], is not only involved in the publication of this edition of the *Thesaurus of ERIC Descriptors* but also publishes the monthly *Current Index to Journals in Education,* which consists of items indexed and abstracted by the ERIC Clearinghouses.

Thus the concept of "centralization vs. decentralization" is not quite one of a federal agency negotiating with the clearinghouses of academia. There is the additional complexity of the private sector of the economy relating to the public sector. That the contracts have in fact been shifted from one firm to another demonstrates the competitive element built into the system.

Ultimately, however, there is little question about the final nature of the "authority." Clearinghouses may be decentralized, potential contractors may compete with actual contractors, but the Office of Education makes the final decisions as to which university or professional association is the site of a given clearinghouse, which firm is to have the contract, and what the terms will be. The point is that the nature of the federal authority behind the "authority list" is twofold. The U.S. Office of Education serves as both a single party to pluralistic terminology negotiations and as the source of overall power through its role of contract initiator, monitor, and renewer.[11]

Guidelines for Using the Thesaurus of ERIC Descriptors

To assist the user in determining the proper descriptors from several approaches, the terminology of the *Thesaurus* is displayed in four sections. The main body, "Descriptors," is actually the Thesaurus of Terms. The other sections serve as indexes to that basic file. Discussed here in order of appearance are the Descriptors (Thesaurus of Terms), the "Rotated Descriptor Display," the "Descriptor Groups," and the "Descriptor Group Display." Each is explained in some detail.

For ease in using the fourth edition of the *Thesaurus,* whether for indexing or searching, two basic conventions employed in it must be explained. First, the descriptors are alphabetized on a "letter-by-letter" basis. For example, "TIME" is separated from "TIME SHARING" by such terms as "TIME BLOCKS," "TIMED TESTS," "TIME FACTORS (LEARNING)" and "TIME PERSPECTIVES"; "ART EXPRESSION" is separated from "ART MATERIALS" by such terms as "ARTICULATION" and "ARTIFICIAL SPEECH." Second, in making a choice between the singular or plural noun forms of descriptors, the general rule to follow is that the plural form will be applied when the proposed term is a "count noun," that is, when one should ask "how many" (as in "LIBRARY NETWORKS"), and the singular form for "mass nouns," that is, when one should ask "how much" (as in "LIBRARY CIRCULATION").

I. Organization of the Thesaurus of ERIC Descriptors: Components

    A. Descriptor List (Thesaurus of Terms)

        Two types of terms appear in the *Thesaurus*—descriptors and synonyms or near synonyms. Descriptors are technically meaningful terms or short phrases that are used to characterize a document and thus serve as both index and search terms. Descriptors perform a dual function in an information storage and retrieval system. First, they permit the indexer to describe the subject elements of a document so that it may be stored in the system for future search and retrieval purposes. Second, they represent the raw material from which the searcher may construct a question for the system to answer. In this sense, the body of descriptors is the communication link between the system itself and its human operators and users.

In the ERIC *Thesaurus,* all descriptors (i.e., valid terms) appear as main entries in boldface capital letters. They are filed alphabetically, letter by letter. Each descriptor is shown with its hierarchical structuring, other cross-references, and scope note, as needed. All cross-references are reciprocal; for example, for each *Use* reference there is a *Used For* reference and for each broader term there is a narrower term. Synonyms or near synonyms of descriptors are printed in boldface capital and lowercase letters (with the exception of acronyms, which are displayed in full capitals). Although synonyms and near synonyms are interfiled as main entries with the descriptors, they may not be used for indexing or as valid search terms.

1. Notations

Five notations are used to structure and display each type of term in the *Thesaurus:* (1) *Use;* (2) *Used For* (*UF*); (3) *Narrower Term* (*NT*); (4) *Broader Term* (*BT*); and (5) Related *Term* (*RT*).

(*a*) A *Use* entry follows synonyms or near synonyms of descriptors, and it directs the user to the preferred descriptor for communicating with the ERIC system.

> *Example:* **Bibliographic Control**
> USE CATALOGING

Ideally there should be as many points of entry to the *Thesaurus* as possible, and therefore there should be as many entry points for a given concept as there are ways to describe that concept. The *Use* entry, then, can extend beyond synonymity to a relationship with a descriptor of near synonymity which has a general conceptual similarity but is not a true synonym.

> *Example:* **Information Retrieval Precision**
> USE RELEVANCE (INFORMATION
> RETRIEVAL)

(*b*) The *Used For* (*UF*) entry appears only under a descriptor for which there is a synonym or near synonym in the *Thesaurus*. It tells the user that the descriptor includes the concept represented by the *UF* entry, and therefore it adds to the user's understanding of the scope of a descriptor which is used for other concepts.

> *Example:* **CATALOGING** 330
> UF   Bibliographic Control

It also tells the user that he cannot accomplish a search by using the *UF* entry.

(*c*) *Narrower Term* (*NT*) denotes a hierarchical relationship between the main descriptor entry and a descriptor which belongs to the same class but is on a lower level of hierarchy: that is, the narrower term is more specific. In other words, a *Narrower Term* is regarded as a subclass of a *Broader Term*.

> *Example:* **INFORMATION RETRIEVAL** 330
> NT   Search Strategies

(*d*) *Broader Term* (*BT*) is the second hierarchical notation and it is the reciprocal of the *Narrower Term* reference. A *BT* entry indicates that the descriptor is of the same class but that it is on a higher level of hierarchy.

> *Example:* **INFORMATION RETRIEVAL** 330
> NT   Search Strategies
> BT   Information Utilization

(*e*) *Related Term* (*RT*) performs two functions, only one of which is concerned with the scope of the main entry. First, a term listed as *RT* clarifies the scope: that is, it provides further definition of a main descriptor. It does this by better describing the context in which the main entry should be interpreted. The second function of *RT* is to alert the user to terms other than the main descriptor in which he may be interested, either as an indexer or as a user of the system. *RT* entries provide the collateral word relationships in a thesaurus that would not ordinarily be apparent if the user were to think only in terms of the hierarchical scheme.

> *Example:* **CATALOGING** 330
> UF   Bibliographic Control

```
                            NT   Indexing
                            BT   Library Technical Processes
                            RT   Book Catalogs
                                 Classification
                                 Information Processing
```

          or
Example: **INDEXING** 330

```
                            UF   Coordinate Indexing
                            NT   Automatic Indexing
                            BT   Cataloging
                            RT   Classification
                                 Information Retrieval
                                 Search Strategies
```

Every hierarchical and collateral entry has a complementary entry elsewhere in the *Thesaurus*. Just as for every *USE* entry, there is a complementary *UF* entry; for every *NT* entry, there is a complementary *BT* entry; conversely, for every *BT* entry, there is a complementary *NT* entry; and for every *RT* entry, there is a complementary *RT* entry. The order in which the notations appear under a descriptor, when appropriate, is as follows:

```
            UF      Used For
            NT      Narrower Term
            BT      Broader Term
            RT      Related Term
```

2. Parenthetical qualifiers

Parenthetical qualifiers follow a number of terms in this *Thesaurus*. Their purpose is to clarify homographs and ambiguities in word meaning and usage, rather than to define descriptors. The homograph and its parenthetical qualifier are considered inseparable in indexing or searching, and they remain together throughout all of the hierarchical and collateral relationships with other descriptors in the *Thesaurus*.

Example: **ARTICULATION (PROGRAM)**
ARTICULATION (SPEECH)
RELEVANCE (EDUCATION)
RELEVANCE (INFORMATION RE-
TRIEVAL)

The use of parentheses in this case should not be confused with the parentheses used in some searching systems to express the logical properties of a search question.

3. Scope Notes

Because of their broad usage in the language or their special usage in fields other than education, some descriptors selected for the *Thesaurus* require a brief statement of their intended usage. In such cases, a scope note has been provided directly beneath the main descriptor entry. It is not intended to be a formal definition, and it appears only when the descriptor is a main entry. It is not carried with the descriptor to other locations in the *Thesaurus*.

> *Example:* **BIBLIOGRAPHIC COUPLING** 330
> SN   Separation of a body of literature into small related groups through correlation of similar sets of references or bibliographies cited

> *or*
> *Example:* **INFORMATION SCIENCE** 330
> SN   Generation, transformation, communication, storage, retrieval, and use of information

B. Rotated Descriptor Display

It became evident in the early stages of the construction of the ERIC *Thesaurus* that the language used by educators required far more utilization of multiword terms than is necessary in the physical sciences. Thus, the *Thesaurus* contains relatively few single-word terms. In using the *Thesaurus,* the researcher or indexer has no common reference point for multiword terms such as "VISUALLY HANDICAPPED" or "HANDICAPPED STUDENTS," even though both are a part of Descriptor Group 240 and other "types" of handicaps are listed, as "MENTALLY HANDICAPPED," "ORTHOPEDICALLY HANDICAPPED." Unlike the "Thesaurus of Terms," where descriptors are alphabetized on a letter-by-letter basis ignoring all spaces between words, the Rotated Descriptor Display, which is actually a KWIC index (*Key Word In Context*), sorts from left to right, considering each word in single order and multiword descriptors as a unit. Thus it serves as an alphabetical index to all significant words that form descriptors in the *Thesaurus* except *USE* references.

This index tends to group related terms generically where they may often be separated by the alphabetical array in the "Thesaurus of Terms," because their filing positions are far apart. When each word of a compound descriptor is rotated and filed together, it is simple to match the words as "HANDICAPPED" to see their complete word forms.

Example:	HANDICAPPED	
ACADEMICALLY	HANDICAPPED	
AURALLY	HANDICAPPED	
	HANDICAPPED	CHILDREN
CUSTODIAL MENTALLY	HANDICAPPED	
LANGUAGE	HANDICAPPED	

```
            MENTALLY  HANDICAPPED
            VISUALLY  HANDICAPPED MOBILITY
            MULTIPLY  HANDICAPPED
       NEUROLOGICALLY  HANDICAPPED
            VISUALLY  HANDICAPPED ORIENTATION
       ORTHOPEDICALLY  HANDICAPPED
         PERCEPTUALLY  HANDICAPPED
          PHYSICALLY  HANDICAPPED
              SPEECH  HANDICAPPED
                      HANDICAPPED STUDENTS
   TRAINABLE MENTALLY  HANDICAPPED
            VISUALLY  HANDICAPPED
```

C. Descriptor Groups

The listing of Descriptor Group categories is arranged alphabetically by each group's three-digit code number and scope note. Cross-references to related Descriptor Groups are given in many scope notes.

> *Example:* **450 RESEARCH**
> Areas and methods of investigation or experimentation having for its aim the discovery of new facts, e.g., Area Studies, Deaf Research, Experimental Programs, Research Methodology, etc.

> *or*

> *Example:* **060 BEHAVIOR**
> Kinds and types of human behavior and factors related to the study of behavior, e.g., Violence, Socially Deviant Behavior, Conditioned Response, Overt Response, etc. See *also* LEARNING AND COGNITION, PSYCHOLOGY, SOCIOLOGY.

D. Descriptor Group Display

The Descriptor Group Display is provided for browsing, for determining descriptor relationships and usage, and for showing related descriptors to aid in structuring new terms for the system. Each Descriptor Group contains the three-digit code number and a list of subject-related descriptors which appear in, and are mutually exclusive to, that group.

> *Example:* **360 OPPORTUNITIES**
> CAREER OPPORTUNITIES
> COMMUNITY BENEFITS
> CULTURAL OPPORTUNITIES
> ECONOMIC OPPORTUNITIES
> EDUCATIONAL OPPORTUNITIES
> EMPLOYMENT OPPORTUNITIES
> HOUSING OPPORTUNITIES

OPPORTUNITIES
RESEARCH APPRENTICESHIPS
RESEARCH OPPORTUNITIES
SOCIAL OPPORTUNITIES
TEACHING BENEFITS
YOUTH OPPORTUNITIES

Examples of typical descriptor structures as they must be displayed are presented in figure 5. Only descriptors actually used for indexing may be included.

```
I.  Descriptor ------------------------ INFORMATION NETWORKS

    Scope Note ------------------------ SN  Information systems linked
                                            for information exchange
                                            through formal communica-
                                            tions

    Broader Term ---------------------- BT  NETWORKS

    Related Term ---------------------- RT  AUDIOVISUAL COMMUNICATION
                                            COMMUNICATION
                                            DIAL ACCESS INFORMATION
                                               SYSTEMS
                                            FACSIMILE COMMUNICATION
                                               SYSTEMS
                                            INFORMATION DISSEMINATION
                                            INFORMATION SERVICES
                                            INFORMATION SYSTEMS
                                            INTERCOMMUNICATION
                                            LIBRARY NETWORKS
                                            TELEPHONE COMMUNICATION
                                               SYSTEMS

II. Descriptor and Parenthetical Qualifier

    Descriptor ------------------------ RELEVANCE (INFORMATION RETRIEVAL)

    Used For -------------------------- UF  Information Retrieval
                                               Precision
                                            Recall Ratio
                                            Relevance Ratio

    Broader Term ---------------------- BT  EVALUATION

    Related Term ---------------------- RT  EVALUATION METHODS
                                            INFORMATION RETRIEVAL
                                            INFORMATION SYSTEMS
                                            PERFORMANCE
                                            RELIABILITY
                                            SEARCH STRATEGIES
                                            SYSTEMS ANALYSIS

III. USE  reference to an acceptable Descriptor

    Descriptor------------------------- Information Retrieval Precision
                                        USE RELEVANCE (INFORMATION
                                           RETRIEVAL)
```

Figure 5
Three examples of typical descriptor structures
displayed in the required format

II. Procedures for New Descriptor Coordination

The decentralized nature of the ERIC system, with subject specialists located at points remote from a central processing site, made it necessary to design and issue formal procedures for the generation, addition, and coordination of new descriptors to be included in the ERIC *Thesaurus*. Rules prepared and approved by the Panel on Educational Terminology outline the requirements that must be met by candidate descriptors before they can become authoritative terms in the *Thesaurus*.

At the clearinghouse level, subject specialists determine the need for a new descriptor by considering the relative frequency of occurrence of a concept in the literature, the relative frequency of its use within the operating system, its relationship to descriptors selected previously, and its technical precision and acceptability. New descriptors must be appraised and considered for inclusion in the *Thesaurus* on the basis of their estimated usefulness in communication, indexing, and retrieval. Subject specialists must be continuously aware of the fact that a candidate descriptor within their fields of interest may have another meaning in other fields. The acceptability of terms can be determined by consulting such references as thesauri, dictionaries, handbooks, and the like.

Using the *Rules for Thesaurus Preparation,* the subject specialist at the clearinghouse prepares an ERIC Descriptor Justification and Data Input Form (DJF), shown in figure 6, for purposes of entering a new term or modifying the scope note and cross-references for an existing descriptor. The candidate term, with its justification and the processed document, are transmitted to the ERIC facility. The DJF is analyzed by the contractor's lexicographer for completeness and validity of generic structure, cross-references, as well as compliance with the PET Rules. Significant changes are negotiated with the clearinghouse by telephone, and questions which cannot be resolved in this manner are referred to the senior lexicographer at Central ERIC. This procedure provides each clearinghouse with current information on proposed changes, reduces the duplication of effort, and offers an opportunity for rebuttal and dialogue within the ERIC system.

III. The Lexicographic Function in Vocabulary Control

The construction and control of the *Thesaurus of ERIC Descriptors* is a decentralized operation involving the personnel and facilities of the various clearinghouses and central lexicography. It is important to note that each clearinghouse works independently, and that its personnel is composed of subject specialists in a particular area of education. The literature of education is multidisciplinary, and therefore the subject specialists are knowledgeable in such areas as

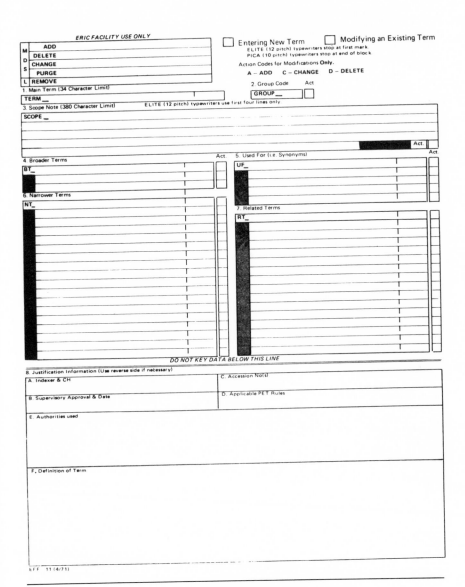

Figure 6
ERIC Descriptor Justification and Data Input Form

science, mathematics, linguistics, psychology, sociology, and so on. Thus, in each subject field the terminology has a specific meaning. If the terms submitted by clearinghouses for incorporation into the *Thesaurus* were without lexicographic analysis, they could be inconsistent, ambiguous, redundant, or unrestrictive. This is the principal problem of a decentralized system; the solution is a central coordination center with authority to analyze and control the development of a thesaurus.

In the ERIC program, central lexicography reviews the structure of candidate descriptors from all subject fields. All terms submitted by clearinghouses are evaluated (1) to maintain consistency; (2) to avoid proliferation; (3) to clarify ambiguities; and (4) to conform to existing rules and guidelines. Brief analyses of these conditions, including examples, problems, and solutions, are relevant here.

A. To Maintain Consistency

Clearinghouses working separately may easily generate inconsistent terminology; for instance, the concepts "academic" and "scholastic" may be considered "near synonyms" for purposes of retrieval. Therefore, the use of both concepts creates a problem of inconsistency.

Example: **Scholastic Failure**
USE   ACADEMIC FAILURE

or

ACADEMIC ACHIEVEMENT
UF   Scholastic Achievement

Problem: The lack of consistency in the terminology means that the chance of locating relevant documents is reduced and processing costs are multiplied. Furthermore, the user must check many unnecessary entries if he is to complete a successful search.

Solution: Central lexicography receives candidate descriptors from the clearinghouses, checks the various reference sources available to determine whether the terms are actually "near synonyms" and, if so, which is the preferred usage. When the decision is made, a precedent is established, a descriptor is selected, and a "Used For" cross-reference is fixed, as in the example above.

B. To Avoid Proliferation

The advantages of avoiding proliferation are twofold: first, it controls the size of the *Thesaurus* by eliminating duplicate or redundant concepts, and second, it increases the effectiveness of the

Thesaurus as a retrieval tool by storing all synonymous terms under one main descriptor.

> *Example:* **INDUSTRIAL ARTS**
> **Industrial Crafts**
> **Practical Skills**
>
> *also*
>
> **INDUSTRIAL EDUCATION**
> **Industrial Instruction**
> **INDUSTRIAL TRAINING**

Problem: If all candidate terms enter the *Thesaurus,* a user searching for information in the field of Industrial Arts and Industrial Education must search all six terms, since they will not be stored together.

Solution: With central control, all candidate terms are available simultaneously, and all are analyzed to determine whether they are synonyms or near synonyms. If this is the case, they may be stored together under the aegis of one descriptor.

C. To Clarify Ambiguities

Experts using a word or group of words to define a particular concept may not be aware that the term may have a different meaning in other subject fields.

> *Example:* A clearinghouse submits the descriptor "TRAVEL TRAINING." In this instance, the term relates to the training of a visually handicapped person to move freely in his environment. This clearinghouse deals with this concept daily, sees no ambiguity in its meaning, and submits it as a candidate for inclusion in the *Thesaurus.*

Problem: A descriptor of this type would also have meaning in other subject areas. For example, a specialist in Vocational Education might well be interested in the training of personnel for a career in the tourist industry. Therefore, in his judgment, the term "TRAVEL TRAINING" might well relate to the training of airline hostesses, reservation agents, and the like. He would channel his search in this direction and thus receive a number of "false drops"—references dealing with the "VISUALLY HANDICAPPED." The cost of such a search would multiply needlessly.

Solution: When the term is submitted to the central control point, the ambiguity may readily be detected, because all clearinghouse documents and résumés are available for reference. After noting the use of this term in other fields, a scope note may be recommended for the purpose of alerting the user to the fact that the concept is restricted to the field of the "VISUALLY HANDICAPPED."

IV. Coordinate Indexing and Multiword Terms

No discussion of the *Thesaurus of ERIC Descriptors* would be complete without some consideration of the principle of coordinate indexing upon which it is based. In contrast to the traditional approach of subject analysis and classification as exemplified by the Library of Congress system, with its numerous subdivisions and inverted headings, coordinate indexing allows separate terms or concepts to be used individually as they are needed for the retrieval of information.

In his article on the role of the thesaurus in education, Dr. Goodman also writes about the "multiword term problem," and again this text is highly significant here:

One of the most difficult tasks facing anyone constructing an indexing scheme is to determine just what it is that he will consider to be the basic elements of his work. The control of synonyms or quasi-synonyms, the problems of preferred usage, the questions of hierarchical relationship, and the neverending mazes of "related terms" are issues conspicuous to anyone who turns the pages of the *Thesaurus*. But at a more basic level than this lies the issue of when to enter a one word descriptor and when to enter a multiword descriptor. Indeed, this is the issue which leads to consideration of the origin of the name "coordinate indexing."

Without going into historical detail, we can reasonably view the approach under consideration as a fundamental departure from the idea of fixing a piece of literature in its place within a logical classification scheme. That is, it is a departure from the slogan "a place for everything, and everything in its place." The "place" for a document under this approach is quite simple: each new piece of literature is simply placed "on top of the pile" in that it is simply given the next available accession number. After it becomes buried in the pile, hopes for finding it are pinned on labeling it with an appropriate number of appropriate descriptive terms. Then, either by listing under a descriptor the numbers of all the documents which have been labeled with that particular descriptor, or by arranging for electronically aided high-speed scanning of all documents in such a way that a desired label will be spotted, retrieval is to take place. Chances of finding just what one is looking for rest mainly on being able to "coordinate" two or more labels, descriptors, in the sense that one is presented with the document numbers which are listed under both of two desired terms (or, in the other sense just mentioned, the document numbers which the scanner has spotted as being associated with both of the two desired terms).

Obviously, however, [this] approach leads to very severe problems. Let us consider just four terms: "college," "students," "teachers," and "part time." If a search were conducted on any two of these, such as "students" and "part time" in order to produce literature on "part time students," the result might involve documents which had been indexed under *"part time"* "teachers" of "college" *"students."* On the other hand, one might search for "college students" and get documents indexed as being about *"college"* "teachers" who taught *"students"* who were "part time." Can literature on "student teachers" be extracted via this scheme? How about "part time college"? The problem is just beginning, for any document that has only *three* of the terms could yield the wrong pair. For example, the request for "college student" would yield not only all documents dealing with "college teachers" and *"part time* students," but also all documents dealing with "college teachers" and *any kind* of students as long as the term "students" appeared as a descriptor. Perhaps when one notes that this illustration allowed one "obvious" multiword descriptor ("part time") from the start, the incredible nature of a pure one word system begins to emerge. Concepts of "leisure *time,*" television "viewing-*time,*" or any kind of *"part,"* could further complicate searches.

A rather wide variety of solutions to such problems have been offered by people interested in retrieving information. Very creative and imaginative approaches have been used to specify the *role* that a term plays in describing a document. Similarly, to avoid false relationships like those just described, efforts have been made to *link* single terms together as they occur as descriptors of a particular document. In fact, work like this on "roles" and "links" at Western Reserve University in the late 1950s and early 1960s contributed to the enthusiasm for specialized information systems that first led to documents proposing that an "ERIC" system be created. . . .

The approach to coordinating terms which is the basis for the *Thesaurus of ERIC Descriptors* was largely the approach used by several federal agencies and by those developing a retrieval system for engineers. The work done at agencies such as the Department of Defense and the Federal Aviation Agency, as well as that done by the Engineers Joint Council, did not attempt to introduce "roles," "links," "facets," or any other elaboration that went beyond allowing multiword terms to be entered into the thesaurus when deemed necessary. The language used by educators, however, seems to have required far more utilization of multiword terms than is necessary in areas drawing more heavily on the physical sciences. The quickest way to see how few single word terms exist in this *Thesaurus* is to examine them as they appear in the "Rotated Descriptor Display". . . .

This proliferation of multiword terms probably did not occur as a matter of policy, although the rules covering multiwords are quite permissive. The rules in question have not changed since October 1966, when they were first presented in the *Rules for Thesaurus Preparation*. The subject is sufficiently important that the relevant passages are shown here (utilizing the system of enumeration employed in the September 1969 version):

1.1.1.1   Descriptors should represent important concepts found in the literature rather than concepts derived independently. They should also reflect the language used in the literature to describe such concepts.

*   *   *   *   *

1.1.1.4   Multiword descriptors (bound terms, precoordinated terms, and others) should be used whenever single-word descriptors cannot describe a concept adequately or provide effective retrieval. Many problems of this type can be solved by the careful application of rule 1.1.1.1 above. The following points should also be considered:

1.1.1.4.1   Use of a multiword descriptor is justified if any of the individual words in the multiword descriptor can combine so frequently with other descriptors as to produce many false coordinations.

1.1.1.4.2   Use of a multiword descriptor to represent a unique concept is justified if the individual words of that multiword term are also unique descriptors which, when coordinated with each other, represent concepts different from the one intended by the multiword term.

Example: **Students**
Teachers
Student Teachers

1.1.1.4.3   If a single-word term (used as a substantive) is so general as to be virtually useless in searching (e.g., **Schools**), consider the use of that term with another term (e.g., **Secondary Schools**).

1.1.1.4.4   Multiword descriptors, like single-word descriptors, must be carefully considered for placement in descriptor hierarchies. . . .

The proper number of multiword terms is partly a question of the extent to which the *Thesaurus* is used as a searching aid. . . . As long as searchers use the *Thesaurus* to develop a sophisticated search strategy, violations in the form of too many multiword terms may make less difference than one might think.

The extensive proliferation of terms which can occur if multiword terms are made the basic indexing units does seem to mean that documents can be described in more "precise" terms than if only more general, single-word, descriptors were used. The cost of this kind of "precision" can be seen in two ways, however. Documents which could have been described by one descriptor may now be described by either or both of two descriptors, or perhaps by even more. For example, it might be dangerous to have the following four descriptors: **Group Tests, Group Intelligence Tests, Group Testing,** and **Group Intelligence Testing.** A searcher might search on one or two of these terms and assume that he had found all the relevant documents. With such a proliferation of multiword terms, the cost can be viewed in terms of relevant documents not found. On the other hand, the cost may be seen in terms of the energy required to perform the more elaborate search made necessary by a level of "precision" necessary so as not to miss relevant documents.

If a searcher makes extensive use of the *Thesaurus* in designing a search strategy, the odds of incurring the "missed document" cost go down, as does the cost of concocting a sophisticated search strategy. Because the *Thesaurus* is extensively cross-referenced, the cost of developing a sophisticated search strategy is less than it would be if one had to exhaustively examine an unstructured list of multiword terms.[12]

Summary

The *Thesaurus of ERIC Descriptors* is the major tool used by subject specialists in the various clearinghouses to accomplish the indexing task. The existence of the *Thesaurus* provides control and consistent use of the vocabulary at any or all phases of system operation. Since, as previously noted, the *Thesaurus* includes generic relationships for the main descriptive terms (broader terms, narrower terms, related terms), it serves as a means of bringing to the attention of the indexer those vocabulary terms which may be employed in making a search for a document and/or to the searcher those vocabulary terms which are likely to have been used by the indexer in describing documents pertinent to the searcher's questions. In its development as an authoritative list of retrieval terms, the ERIC *Thesaurus* serves as an excellent example of an up-to-date, manipulable vocabulary. Students of education and information science should view this thesaurus as an illustration of the type of language control which is essential to the operation of an information retrieval system.

SAMPLE EXERCISES

Problem: In 1968/69, school districts in the State of California spent an average of $815 per pupil on educational programs, while

Mississippi school districts expended about $503 per pupil for similar training. What studies are available in the ERIC file which would give some accounting for such sharp differences in the financing of these programs for school children?

Instructions: Using the *Thesaurus*, find and list those descriptors which seem relevant to this problem. Show at least two alternative approaches to rephrasing this question.

Alternative I:

Step 1. Enter the *Thesaurus* at "COSTS."

COSTS ---NT---→ Student Costs

COSTS ---RT---→ Expenditure Per Student

Step 2. STUDENT COSTS ---NT---→ Tuition

STUDENT COSTS ---RT---→ Unit Costs

Step 3. EXPENDITURE PER STUDENT ---RT---→ School District Spending

Step 4. TUITION ---BT---→ Student Costs

Relevant Descriptors: EXPENDITURE PER STUDENT
SCHOOL DISTRICT SPENDING

Alternative II:

Step 1. Enter *Thesaurus* at "Finance." *See* note, USE EDUCATIONAL FINANCE

Step 2. EDUCATIONAL FINANCE ---RT---→ Expenditure Per Student

EDUCATIONAL FINANCE ---RT---→ School District Spending

EDUCATIONAL FINANCE ---RT---→ School Funds

Step 3. SCHOOL DISTRICT SPENDING ---RT---→ Expenditure Per Student

Step 4. SCHOOL FUNDS ---RT---→ School Support

Step 5. SCHOOL SUPPORT ---RT---→ School Funds

Relevant Descriptors: EDUCATIONAL FINANCE
EXPENDITURE PER STUDENT
SCHOOL SUPPORT
SCHOOL FUNDS
SCHOOL DISTRICT SPENDING

Alternative III:

Step 1. Enter *Thesaurus* at "School Finance." *See* note, USE EDUCATIONAL FINANCE.

Step 2. EDUCATIONAL FINANCE ---RT---→ Expenditure Per Student

Relevant Descriptors: EDUCATIONAL FINANCE
EXPENDITURE PER STUDENT

Alternative IV:

Step 1. Enter *Thesaurus* at "State." *See* note, USE STATE PRO-
GRAMS

Step 2. At STATE PROGRAMS, note Descriptor Group Code
Number 230. Proceed to Descriptor Groups section of
Thesaurus and read scope note for Group 230, Government.
Relevance of descriptors in this group is doubtful. However,
to be certain, proceed to Descriptor Group Display and
check list of descriptors included under Group 230.

Step 3. As a further check to this approach, enter Rotated Descriptor
Display at term "State." Note various uses and combinations of that term. None appears relevant to this problem.

Notes

1. Kenneth D. Carroll, *Survey of Scientific-Technical Tape Services* (New
York: American Institute of Physics, 1970).
2. U.S. Library of Congress, Subject Cataloging Division, *Subject Headings
Used in the Dictionary Catalogs of the Library of Congress,* 7th ed.
(Washington, D.C.: Library of Congress, 1966).
3. *Sears List of Subject Headings,* 10th ed. (New York: Wilson, 1972).
4. John R. Sharp, *Some Fundamentals of Information Retrieval* (London:
Andre Deutsch, 1965), p. 68.
5. Sharp, p. 133.
6. Gordon C. Barhydt and Charles T. Schmidt, *Information Retrieval
Thesaurus of Education Terms* (Cleveland: The Press of Case Western
Reserve Univ., 1968), p. v.
7. "Thesaurus of ERIC Descriptors Guidelines," *ERIC Operating Manual*
(Bethesda, Md.: ERIC Processing and Reference Facility, LEASCO Systems and Research Corp., 1971), Section 3.4.4–2.
8. *Thesaurus of ERIC Descriptors,* 4th ed. (New York: Macmillan Information, 1972).
9. Students of information science who are interested in this method of
classification are referred to: Gordon C. Barhydt and Charles T. Schmidt,
Information Retrieval Thesaurus of Education Terms (Cleveland: The
Press of Case Western Reserve Univ., 1968).
10. *Thesaurus,* p. 319.
11. Frederick Goodman, "The Role and Function of the Thesaurus in Education," in *Thesaurus of ERIC Descriptors,* 4th ed. (New York: Macmillan
Information, 1972), p. *vii–viii*.
12. *Thesaurus,* p. *xiii–xiv*.

4

The Science
and Art
of Indexing

Introduction

Information systems are complex agencies with a variety of components performing in special relationships to provide information. In the case of an information retrieval system, this means that the system must be capable of retrieving documents in answer to specific subject requests. One of this system's most essential tools is the index, the list of words used to describe the characteristics of documents in the file and to provide the language in which requests for information from that file must be phrased. In this instance, therefore, the principal index is the subject index, and the process of indexing involves not only that of making decisions about the subject matter of the document, but also that of regarding the document in the light of the types of users who may be expected to benefit from its contents.

For purposes of explanation and continuity, frequent references to the characteristics of the ERIC information base, and the indexing procedures used with it, are interspersed throughout this chapter. In this regard, "ERIC Guidelines for Indexing," *ERIC Operating Manual,* Section 3.4.3, 1971 edition, was the primary source of information.[1] However, the reader is again reminded that the detailed use of ERIC is as a model, whereby the principles and procedures of indexing may be more readily explained and understood.

Coordinate Indexing and Subject Searching

Document processing in the ERIC system is based upon the principle of coordinate indexing, the underlying purpose of which (as in other indexing programs) is to assign "tags" or "handles" to concepts in the literature so that they can be retrieved. Instead of indicating one or two subjects covering the entire content, as is the usual procedure with the subject-cataloging of books, those working with report literature must attach a term to every significant concept in the report, much like an index in a book. In coordinate indexing for the ERIC program, the indexing terms (descriptors) are assigned by the indexer with the intent that they will be used either together or separately in the search process. Thus, the indexer must know what combinations of terms should be made, but it is the searcher, looking for reports on a specific subject, who will actually make the combinations, simply by looking for all terms covering the topic of his interest among those assigned to each document.

As described in chapter 3, in many cases the relationships between terms have already been recognized by the combining of concepts before index-ing, such as, "PART-TIME STUDENTS" or "TEACHER EDUCA-TION." In other words, some descriptors in the ERIC *Thesaurus* have been "precoordinated," thus eliminating the need for multiple combina-tions of subject headings and reducing conflicts in search techniques. Whether descriptors are precoordinated or postcoordinated, that is, com-bined at the time of indexing or of searching, the essence of their purpose is to provide multiple access points to multifaceted documents.

A brief illustration of a search strategy in an information retrieval system is important here. A searcher may want documents on "TEACH-ING METHODS" for the "CULTURALLY DISADVANTAGED." He examines the indexes, *Research in Education* and *Current Index to Journals in Education,* for the reports to which these two terms have been assigned. He may decide, upon looking at the results of a preliminary search, that some documents were not uncovered. Therefore, to find more documents (increase recall), he may add a term and conduct another search on "TEACHING METHODS" for "CULTURALLY DISADVANTAGED" or for "SOCIALLY DISADVANTAGED." In fact, he may *broaden* the search on both terms and structure his question as follows: "TEACHING METHODS" or "TEACHING TECHNIQUES," and "CULTURALLY DISADVANTAGED" or "SOCIALLY DISADVANTAGED." This will result in the retrieval of all documents assigned to either of the descriptors

"TEACHING METHODS" or "TEACHING TECHNIQUES" and either "CULTURALLY DISADVANTAGED" or "SOCIALLY DISADVAN-TAGED." *Or,* if he receives too many irrelevant documents in his search, he may *narrow* the search (increase relevance). For example, if the searcher starts with "TEACHING" and "DISADVANTAGED," he may substitute the terms "TEACHING METHODS" and "CULTURALLY DISADVANTAGED." Thus adjustments can be made to include more or fewer documents by adding or dropping terms or by using more specific descriptors. This aspect of search theory is discussed in detail in chapter 6.

The main purpose of in-depth coordinate indexing, therefore, is to provide effective retrieval of relevant information as efficiently and inexpensively as possible. While in-depth, postcoordinate indexing is initially more expensive than the limited number of subject headings librarians traditionally assign to documents, it provides faster and far more precise subject access to information, since the index terms represent more specific and detailed descriptions of the subjects in the documents.

Indexing in ERIC

The process of indexing for ERIC is similar to that used in any information system; that is, the indexer chooses concepts to be indexed and then translates those concepts into the language of the system. However, before launching into indexing, ERIC personnel must be aware of the following special problems of this multidisciplinary system: (1) the design of the ERIC network and the interests of its users; (2) the methods of subject retrieval; and (3) the nature of the literature of education. The first two problems have been dealt with elsewhere in this book, but some discussion of the nature of the literature of education is warranted here.

The Nature of the Literature

The "ERIC Guidelines for Indexing," as presented in the *ERIC Operating Manual,* include the following statement in regard to the types of documents in the literature of education:

> Although the field comprises many subjects and is itself dependent upon and derived from many other disciplines, its literature is homogeneous in its primary purpose and, to a large extent, in the uses to which it is put. It takes many forms, however. This makes the task of representing its content consistently by index terms a complicated one. Many information systems deal mainly with research studies, or report literature or journal articles. The ERIC system deals with all kinds of "important and significant" educational documents, regardless of the format of their publication, the nature of the

methods used in the study, or the experimental or discursive style of the inquiry.[2]

Indexing Tools

The standard tools for the indexer in an information retrieval system are the following: (1) a thesaurus; (2) rules for adding new terms into the thesaurus; (3) dictionaries, glossaries, and subject-matter textbooks to help the indexer arrive at acceptable *new* and significant terms; and (4) authority lists indicating geographic locations, the correct form of project names, and the like.

The *Thesaurus of ERIC Descriptors* is the principal tool used by the subject specialists in the various clearinghouses to accomplish indexing tasks. The existence of the *Thesaurus* provides both control and consistent use of the vocabulary at any or all phases of the system's operation. As described in chapter 3, the *Thesaurus* includes generic relationships for the main descriptive terms; that is, broader terms, narrower terms, and related terms, thereby bringing to the attention of the indexer those vocabulary terms which might be used in searching for a document, and/or suggesting to the searcher those terms which might be used by the indexer in describing documents.

Another useful tool in the ERIC system is the *Term Usage Statistical Report,* which is available after the annual cumulation of *Research in Education.* The *Report* contains an alphabetical listing of descriptors with the ED accession numbers of the documents to which they have been assigned. In other words, the *Statistical Report* reveals the number of times that a descriptor has been used as an indexing term. The importance of this tool at the searching stage is discussed in chapter 7.

Indexing Techniques

Examining the Document

Indexing begins with an examination of the document. Depending upon the indexer's experience and the nature of the report, one or more readings of the document may be necessary before familiarity with its contents is assured. The indexer must establish his own frame of reference for a given document. First of all, he examines it for certain basic characteristics, such as its source (author and sponsoring institution), its publication date and present timeliness, and its format and organization. He must also determine the document's relationship to the information system and its potential audience. Next, the contents of the document must be analyzed. A technical report is usually written following the sequence in which the work was performed and the results recorded. It is customary for the author or investigator to present the following information: (1) title; (2) abstract; (3) introduction, including the historical and theoretical support for his work; (4) description of the methodology and materials used; (5) discussion; (6) results; (7) illustrative materials, such as charts, graphs, diagrams, and the like; (8) conclusions; (9) summary; (10) index; and (11) references.

In analyzing its subject content, the indexer may examine the document's parts in a more journalistic sequence; that is, by scanning the title, abstract, summary, conclusions, references, introduction, methodology, discussion, illustrations, and results. As he studies the document's contents, the indexer should verify his own interpretation of each section by comparing the abstract with the title, the summary with the abstract, the conclusions with the summary, and so on, until he is familiar with the contents of the report.

Application of the principles described above has been directed primarily towards the indexing of technical reports. However, the literature which is processed into ERIC exists in many forms, thereby complicating systematic analysis. When the structure of technical reports is compared with other forms of documents, a parallel scheme for analysis becomes available, thus providing more consistency both in analysis and indexing (*see* fig. 7).

Identifying Indexable Information

The primary consideration in identifying indexable information in a document lies in the straightforward question, "What is the document about?" ERIC documents usually contain the following elements or concepts of information: population concepts, activities or action concepts, methodology and material concepts, and educational curriculum concepts.

Population concepts include the activities of a group or an individual and any descriptive terms concerning age, involvement in study or program, grade level or occupation, intelligence or ability, physical or emotional characteristics, socioeconomic characteristics, race, religion, or nationality.

Activities or action concepts include teaching, testing, experimentation and the like. Examples of *methodology and materials concepts* are language laboratories, programmed tests, and filmstrips. Usually a decision must be made as to whether the document is concerned with the activity, the methodology and/or materials, or both the activity and the methodology or materials. In some instances, the activity and the methodology might be represented by the same concept. For example, is a given document about testing, or is it about the testing methods and/or tests used, or is it actually concerned with testing and its methods or materials? If it is about

Document Forms	BIBLIOGRAPHIC STRUCTURE										
	*1	2	6	7	8	10	9	4	3	5	11
Technical (Research) Reports	Title	Abstract	Introduction	Methodology Materials	Discussion	Results	Illustrations	Conclusion	Summary	References	Index
Project Description	Title	Abstract	Introduction	Methodology Materials	Objectives	Objectives	Illustrations			References	
Program Report	Title	Abstract	Introduction	Methodology Materials	Discussion	Results	Illustrations	Conclusion	Summary	References	
Curriculum Guides	Title	Table of Contents	Introduction	Methodology Materials			Illustrations			References	Index
Popular Books	Title	Table of Contents	Foreword, Preface, Introduction	Text	Text		Illustrations		Text		
Professional Textbooks, Manuals	Title	Table of Contents	Foreword, Preface, Introduction	Text	Text	Text	Illustrations	Text	Text	References	Index
Dissertations	Title	Abstract	Introduction		Discussion	Objectives	Illustrations	Conclusions	Summary	References	

* Suggested sequence for Review

Figure 7

Comparison of document forms and structure

testing, making only slight mention of methods and specific tests, then it should be indexed at "TESTING." If it is about the development or use of a specific kind of test, such as aptitude tests, then it should be indexed at "APTITUDE TESTS," not at "TESTING." If, however, the document is about testing, and various aptitude tests were used, it should be indexed at "TESTING" as well as at the specific names of aptitude tests for which data and results were presented in the document.

Education curriculum concepts, that is, the subjects or concepts which are being administered, taught, or measured, form the fourth category of indexable information often found in ERIC documents. Examples are arithmetic, history, learning disabilities, reading, and spatial perception, among others. Here again, those concepts which are actively described in the document comprise the indexable information. For example, if a teaching method is used for arithmetic, and this is reported and described in detail, the document should be indexed at "ARITHMETIC" along with terms describing the method, the persons being taught, and so forth. However, if a document mentions that this method might also be used for teaching music, but does not describe this use of the method, then the document should not be indexed at "MUSIC."

After the concepts have been selected according to the above categories, they should be reexamined along with the document. In order to qualify as indexable information, the concepts should fulfill certain basic requirements with respect to the document.

To what extent is the document about a candidate concept? Mere mention of any concept within a document does not provide indexable information. If the concept was a reason for the document to be written, or if, without the concept, the document would either not exist or be significantly altered, then the concept is indexable information.

What generic level of the concept is the document about? The concept should be represented as generically as necessary, but also as specifically as possible, according to the use and meaning in the document. For example, a document entitled *Guidelines for the Referral of Children Who are Suspected or Known to be Exceptional* may describe and define the crippled and health-impaired, deaf, blind, partially seeing, emotionally disturbed and socially maladjusted, educable mentally handicapped, trainable mentally handicapped, and multiply handicapped, as well as the gifted. This document should be retrievable through the generic concepts, "EXCEPTIONAL CHILDREN" and "HANDICAPPED CHILDREN," as well as through each specific area of exceptionality mentioned above. Further examination of the document's content may indicate that a user interested in the visually handicapped, for example, could find this document's information very useful. Also, a user interested in general information on all types of exceptional children would find this document of value. Therefore, this document should be indexed under both generic and specific concepts.

At all times, the indexer must try to think in terms of the system's information user: Would a person who is searching a store of information for documents about a given concept be satisfied to retrieve this document? Would it fulfill his information needs? Would he be disappointed if he were notified of this document because it contained a relatively small amount of information on his subject? It is important to remember that the purpose of indexing a document should always be for its retrievability, rather than its storage.

Identifiers

Proper names of persons, geographical locations, trade names, and the like may also be a part of a document's indexable information. These terms, called *identifiers,* usually cannot be structured into the *Thesaurus of ERIC Descriptors.* Some categories and examples of identifiers follow:

Acronyms (ERIC; MARC; PERT)
Assistance programs (Head Start, Work Incentive Program)
Coined terminology (New Left; New Deal)
Community organizations (New York Urban Corps; Community Chest)
Educational organizations (National Education Association; Teacher Corps)
Equipment names and numbers (Kodak Ektagraphic 8 Camera; Stromberg
    Carlson 4020 Microfilm Recorder)
Geographic names (Stockholm; Nebraska)
Manufacturers (Eastman Kodak; International Business Machines)
Projects (Taba Curriculum Project; Detroit Great Cities Project)
Tests (Stanford-Binet; Rorschach)
Trade names (IBM 360 65; Xerox).

The selection of identifiers should be made on the same basis as the selection of indexing concepts. If the document contains sufficient information about an identifier to justify the document's retrieval by searching for that identifier, then the identifier is indexable information. For example, a document which reports on research that exploited Piaget's theory of concept formation is not actually concerned with Piaget's theory per se. However, the inclusion of "PIAGET'S THEORY" as an identifier can be useful as a retrieval term in a machine-search because someone may want to know the various applications of Piaget's theory. At present, identifiers do not appear in any of the published indexes in the report résumé section where they occur with the descriptors.

Levels of Generality and Specificity

The question of how specifically a concept should be indexed is difficult to answer in any information system, and particularly so in ERIC. In general, documents should be indexed at the level of specificity of the document in hand. This is a fundamental principle of coordinate indexing. For example, if a document refers to handicapped children, the appropriate (precoordinated) term is "HANDICAPPED CHILDREN," not "CHILDREN" and "HANDICAPPED." However, if the document refers to all kinds of children, and handicapped children does not stand out as an obvious concept, then "CHILDREN" would be the appropriate term. If there is general information on children and specific information on handicapped children, then both "CHILDREN" and "HANDICAPPED CHILDREN" are suitable descriptors.

There are several situations when this question of generality and specificity must be carefully considered by the indexer.

1. The document discusses a concept at both a general and specific level; for instance, a document describing intelligence tests in general, as well as specific tests in about equal detail.
2. The document discusses a specific concept (species), but the indexer feels that the document adds useful information to the body of knowledge about the general concept (genus); for example, a document giving details about the Wechsler Adult Intelligence Scale also includes substantial information about intelligence tests.
3. The document discusses many specifics of a general concept (genus), but none in "sufficient" detail to merit the indexing of each specific concept, such as a document comprising an inventory of intelligence tests but with little information on specific tests.

With reference to (1) above, an indexer would consider, for example, both the concept "INTELLIGENCE TESTS" and the identifier, "DETROIT ADVANCED INTELLIGENCE TESTS," as indexable terms. If there is a sufficient amount of information worth indexing (always a matter of judgment) about both general and specific concepts, both are indexed.

In the case of (2) above, the indexer would also index, at the general level, any specific concept which he judges should be retrievable at the broader level as well as at the specific level, even if the general concept is not discussed per se. For example, an extensive description of the Wechsler Adult Intelligence Scale (WAIS) should be indexed by "INTELLIGENCE TESTS," as well as by an identifier, the name of the test. If the ERIC system covered only the literature of educational tests and measurements, this guideline might not be given. However, since ERIC users are likely to be interested in the entire area of tests at varying levels of specificity, this document should be made accessible at a reasonably general level; that is "INTELLIGENCE TESTS," not "TESTS," and at the specific level of the test name as well.

The third area, (3) above, is the most difficult. The indexer must develop a "feel" for what is sufficient or reasonable information about a concept that makes it indexable. Experience in indexing and in reviewing search results will be helpful here. An example may better illustrate this problem. Among other facts, a given study describes the population of persons attending a sequence of conferences. In tabular form it lists the age, sex, educational level, and rate of attendance. The indexer decides that such background information is not significant enough to index specifically, since none of those factors appears to be a variable in the study. Therefore, this group of concepts is indexed at a generic level as "PARTICIPANT CHARACTERISTICS."

Translating Concepts into the Language of the System

When the concepts in a document have been identified and listed as candidates for descriptors, they must be translated into the language of the *Thesaurus*. Each candidate term must be compared with the descriptors to determine (1) whether an exact equivalent is available in the *Thesaurus;* (2) whether a synonym or near synonym is in the *Thesaurus;* (3) whether a broader term in the *Thesaurus* is adequate for retrieval; (4) whether two or more terms in the *Thesaurus* can be coordinated for retrieval; or (5) whether it is necessary to introduce a new term.

The descriptor section of the *Thesaurus* must be examined to determine whether a particular term is useful or whether a narrower, broader, or related term should be considered. The Rotated Descriptor Display is particularly helpful in this situation. On finding the terms in the *Thesaurus,* often the indexer can only approximate the original concept. Again, its usefulness to the searcher is a basic criterion to follow in selecting a descriptor. The indexer must strive for consistent and exhaustive coverage of each document, using the greatest possible degree of specificity in the selection of descriptors.

Major and Minor Descriptors

When all indexable concepts have been selected and translated into the language of the ERIC *Thesaurus,* the indexer must examine his work to designate the "major" and "minor" descriptors of the document. In general, there are two purposes in ERIC for designating certain descriptors as major (those tagged with an asterisk) and others as minor. The first is to point out the chief, or "major," concepts of a document. The second is to provide subject access to the documents listed in *Research in Education* through the subject index of each issue. The ERIC rule is that at least one, but no more than five, descriptors must be designated as "major" for each document. The point of this rule is to provide the user of RIE with at least one subject route to each document, and to limit the size of the Subject Index to a manageable level.

Certain problems may emerge at this point, for the distinction between major and minor terms could result in a conflict between choosing the principal subject of a document and seeing that descriptor as a useful access point in the Subject Index of RIE. In its traditional hard-copy format, *Research in Education* is designated as a current-awareness service or a general search device for quick scanning. It is not designed for exhaustive manual retrospective searching. That is the function of the computerized data base, where the full power of coordinate indexing and machine searching may be utilized. Therefore, indexers in the ERIC system must realize that, in addition to designating the major concepts of a document and providing subject access to RIE, major descriptors may also be used to represent the general class or subject area to which a document belongs.

In making the distinction between major and minor descriptors, the indexer should carefully consider these questions:

1. Have all significant concepts been indexed, either by one descriptor or by two, allowing for postcoordination at the time of search?
2. If so, which descriptors best denote the major subjects discussed?
3. Are these major descriptors likely to be the most useful retrieval points for the users of RIE?
4. Has the choice of major terms achieved some harmony among these three factors: (a) terms at the level of specificity of the document; (b) terms best descriptive of the subject of the document as a whole; (c) terms providing a class description likely to communicate usefully to the user?

This process clearly indicates that the indexer has two roles to play: one as the describer of the content of a document, and the other as the hypothetical user of ERIC's services, particularly *Research in Education*. To play both roles well, the indexer must be as sensitive to the broad purposes of the ERIC network as he is to the demands for subject representation of documents by the process of indexing.

New Descriptors

Based on the indexer's substantive knowledge of the clearinghouse subject area, concepts in documents are analyzed and expressed as descriptors, and then translated to conform with the language in the *Thesaurus of ERIC Descriptors*.

Any new concept which is not covered by the *Thesaurus* must be carefully appraised when considered for addition to that vocabulary. During this appraisal, the subject specialist in the clearinghouse must always consider the possibility that he may be dealing with new synonyms. If synonymity is ruled out, the term then becomes a candidate descriptor, based on the subject specialist's expertise, the rules of the Panel on Educational Terminology, and the support found in dictionaries, handbooks and other reference materials. Detailed procedures whereby a new term is incorporated into the vocabulary of the ERIC system are discussed in chapter 3.

Review

After the indexer has selected descriptors from the *Thesaurus,* and determined which are major and minor terms, he should review the indexing accomplishments with the following questions in mind:

1. Do the major terms represent the chief emphasis of the document?
2. Are the major terms reflected in the abstract, so that there is no question about their relevance?
3. Are the possibilities for "false drops" (false coordinations) minimal?
4. Do the descriptors reflect all of the important concepts in the document?
5. Can the terms be constructed in a narrative form so as to give a complete and accurate picture of the document (such as, "The overall theme of the document is 'CLASSROOM RESEARCH.' Specifically, the program reported in this document is concerned with producing 'AUDIOVISUAL AIDS' which will be applicable to 'TEACHER EDUCATION,' " etc.)?

The responsibility for ultimate retrieval rests in the hands of the indexer, and he must be concerned that the terms he has selected can be used to effectively retrieve the information in the document.

Summary

One of the important operations in information retrieval is indexing. The principal uses of indexing are either to structure an item of information for retrieval, or to specify distinct pieces of usable data. In an information retrieval system, the counterpart of indexing is the searching process. Coordinate indexing is a generic indexing technique which, in the case of the ERIC system, analyzes documents resulting in a set of terms or concepts. These concepts are arranged in a controlled vocabulary known as the *Thesaurus of ERIC Descriptors.* When such subject lists are developed to the point that they are readily manipulable by both the indexer and the searcher, the communications aspect of the system has been firmly established.

Notes

1. "ERIC Guidelines for Indexing," *ERIC Operating Manual* (Bethesda, Md.: ERIC Processing and Reference Facility, LEASCO Systems and Research Corp., 1971), Section 3.4.3.
2. "ERIC Guidelines for Indexing," Section 3.4.3–8.

part two

Computer Searching: Principles and Strategies

5

Binary
Numeration

Introduction

Prior to discussing some of the techniques of computer searching, it will be useful to examine the fundamental communications alphabet in which machine operations are performed, namely the binary system of numeration. To continue the metaphor, the binary system is an alphabet rather than a "language" in that there is more than one method of working in binary notation, just as there is more than one language which uses the notational system known as the roman alphabet. A good grasp of the fundamentals of binary notation and arithmetic is an asset to librarians more for their help in understanding how computers operate, and indeed for their significance in the study of information transfer generally, than as an everyday working tool. Even computer programmers are seldom called upon to use binary arithmetic. For the librarian, however, the binary system has a special interest because it reveals something fundamental about the structure of information: the *binary digit* ("bit") is, in fact, the most basic unit of recordable information. It takes approximately eight binary digits to represent any normal character (a letter, number, punctuation mark, special symbol, and the like) and to comprehend this relationship is to gain not only a better appreciation of the computer and its operations upon data, but also a fresh insight into our existing conceptual units of information such as the word, the book, the page, the catalog entry, and even the library.

Binary Notation

This is a method of counting in units of two, instead of the customary ten. It is built entirely on a base of two symbols, "0" and "1," as if humans happened to have two fingers instead of ten, or had chosen to employ their two arms as the foundation of the counting system. As in conventional arithmetic, which is built upon a base of ten symbols and is therefore a decimal system, numbers are constructed by the positional device of moving a digit one space to the left for each higher order of the base.

In the binary system, zero is represented by "0" and one by "1," but there the pictorial similarity with decimal numbers ends. Instead of amassing ten of a set or class, calling it a "set of ten," and indicating this by placing a "1" in the second column, binary counting works by accumulating just two, calling it a "set of two," and shifting left a space. In any positional numbering system (and there are others besides decimal and binary), the shift is governed by the number of symbols in the system. In decimal arithmetic the next leftward shift must occur when, and only when, ten of these "sets of ten" have been counted; that is, at one "hundred." In binary, a third figure becomes necessary upon reaching two of the "sets of two"; that is, at one "four."

Thus, whereas the symbol group "10" in decimal arithmetic represents ten (a ten plus zero units), in binary it stands for two (a two plus zero units) and should therefore only be read, written, and pronounced as "two." Likewise "100," a decimal hundred, is of course a binary four. It will be clear to the reader that while the decimal system utilizes powers, or exponents, of ten, the binary system is constructed in powers of two, which gives it great appeal to mathematicians, logicians, and others who work with numbers. The powers of two form a doubling sequence (2, 4, 8, 16, and so on), since the factor being exponentiated is two.

It is because the only digits encountered in any given position are "0" and "1" that binary notation is so ideally suited to the electronic computer, and vice versa. Electronic equipment characteristically operates in one of two states—*on* or *off* (the computer is therefore referred to as a "two state" or "bistable" device)—and these states can be unambiguously equated to the two binary symbols. For example, to write a "1" into a particular recording space on tape, disk, or in the main memory, current is turned on; to write a "0" it is switched off. This simple operation is the basis for

Decimal Notation	Binary Notation
1	1
2	10
3	11
4	100
5	101
6	110
7	111
8	1000
16	10000
32	100000

Figure 8
Binary notation

almost all that the computer does, and it is a good antidote for cybernetic fears and fantasies to keep this fact in mind. Figures 8 and 9 illustrate the way the notation works.

Before proceeding to a discussion of the rules for using the binary "alphabet" of "0" and "1," it is worth stressing how completely the digital computer, surely one of the most awesome inventions in human history, is dependent upon this fundamental binary simplicity. Communicating with a modern digital computer is becoming—although not as rapidly as some enthusiasts predicted—an increasingly natural process. This is, of course, to be welcomed, as it vastly enhances the computer's utility by permitting people with little or no special training to work with it. But it is crucial, both to an individual's ability to perform specific tasks on the computer, and to his general appreciation of what computers can and cannot do, to realize that communication at this level (sometimes called the man-machine interface), even when the machine's speed and flexibility gives the appearance that it is thinking and conversing on its own, is merely the topmost layer in a highly complex hierarchy of code systems which ultimately reduce all the symbols of ordinary communication to a series of electromagnetic impulses. Some of these layers are illustrated in figure 10; most of them are purely technical matters of no concern here. But at the lowest level of this hierarchy, the binary code is usually found.

Binary Arithmetic

Binary arithmetic is increasingly emphasized in modern mathematics texts for children, which attempt to inculcate a general facility to work in number systems constructed in bases other than ten. Binary is the simplest

The Decimal Number System

Thousands	Hundreds	Tens	Units
1000	100	10	1
$10\times10\times10$	10×10	10×1	1
10^3	10^2	10^1	1

Thus: 6   3   4   7

Equals: (6×10^3) + (3×10^2) + (4×10^1) + $7(1)$

Which is: six thousands plus three hundreds plus four tens plus seven ones

The Binary Number System

Thirty-twos	Sixteens	Eights	Fours	Twos	Units
32	16	8	4	2	1
$2\times2\times2\times2\times2$	$2\times2\times2\times2$	$2\times2\times2$	2×2	2×1	1
2^5	2^4	2^3	2^2	2^1	1

Thus: 1   0   1   1   0   1

Equals: (1×2^5) + (0×2^4) + (1×2^3) + (1×2^2) + (0×2^1) + (1×1) = 45

Which is: a thirty-two plus an eight plus a four plus a one.

Figure 9
Binary number system

of these other than a number system having a base of only one symbol (which is merely a new name for the oldest of all number systems, the straightforward tally system, $1 + 1 + 1$, and so on). The performance of arithmetic operations in the binary system is not, however, the central concern here, as it has no direct influence upon the librarian's ability to function as an information expert in the computerized search process. But it is helpful to have at least a sense of how binary arithmetic works, and this section is therefore a brief outline of the four basic operations: addition, subtraction, multiplication, and division, beginning with the method for converting decimal numbers to binary, and vice versa.

Conversion

This is done by successively dividing by two the number to be converted into binary form. Either the division will be exact or there will be a re-

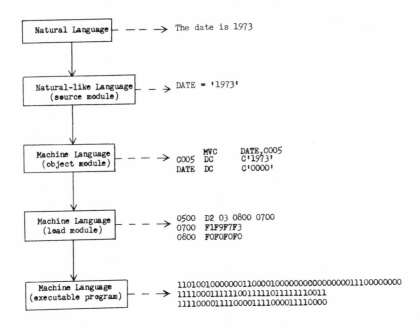

| Natural Language | — — → The date is 1973 |

| Natural-like Language (source module) | — → DATE = '1973' |

| Machine Language (object module) | — — → |

```
          MVC    DATE,C005
C005  DC         C'1973'
DATE  DC         C'0000'
```

| Machine Language (load module) | — — → |

```
0500  D2 03 0800 0700
0700  F1F9F7F3
0800  F0F0F0F0
```

| Machine Language (executable program) | — — → |

```
110100100000001100001000000000000000000011100000000
11110001111110011111011111110011
1111000011110001111000011110000
```

Note: This is intended to be a logical schematic only; it does not necessarily portray the actual sequence of operations in any one type of computer.

Figure 10

Transforming natural language into electronic impulses

mainder of one. In either case, the remainder should be tallied in a separate column, as in the first example.

The resulting column of remainders is then read upward—"100101"— and this is the binary form of the number required. A moment's thought will show why this is correct: the number of positions ("sets of two") a binary number possesses is a function of how many times that number is divisible by two. The first digit of a binary number, in the "units" place to the far right, registers the result of the first attempt to divide by two. Thus, this is the digit appearing at the top of the remainder column.

Converting a binary number to decimal is a process of ascertaining how many powers of two are represented by the number, as indicated by the number of positions it possesses. The rightmost digit (the position for the "units") is naturally omitted from the count, since it can only be zero or

Example: 37

	Remainder
$37 \div 2 = 18$	1
$18 \div 2 = 9$	0
$9 \ \div 2 = 4$	1
$4 \ \div 2 = 2$	0
$2 \ \div 2 = 1$	0
$1 \ \div 2 = 0$	1

one. It is then merely a matter of multiplying out the powers of two corresponding to the binary positions containing the symbol "1," and adding them together.

Example: 100101. Six positions indicate five powers of two:

$$(1 \times 2^5) + (0 \times 2^4) + (0 \times 2^3) + (1 \times 2^2) + (0 \times 2^1) + (1 \times 1)$$
$$= 32 + 0 + 0 + 4 + 0 + 1 = 37$$

The arithmetic operations of addition, subtraction, multiplication and division are carried out using essentially the same procedures as for decimal numbers.

Addition. The basic possibilities are:

$$0 + 0 = 0$$
$$0 + 1 = 1$$
$$1 + 0 = 1$$
$$1 + 1 = 0 \ (0 \text{ with 1 carried to the left})$$

Example:

	22	10110
	+5	+101
	27	11011

Subtraction. The basic possibilities are:

$$0 - 0 = 0$$
$$0 - 1 = 1 \ (1 \text{ with 1 carried from the left})$$
$$1 - 0 = 1$$
$$1 - 1 = 0$$

Example:

	13	1101
	−7	−0111
	6	0110

Note that in the third column, $1 - 1$ does not give the customary 0; because of the necessary carry into column two, the 1 on the top line has become 0. Since column three is now in fact $0 - 1 = 1$, this produces a further carry from column four, which then reads $0 - 0 = 0$.

Multiplication. The basic possibilities are:

$$0 \times 0 = 0$$
$$0 \times 1 = 0$$
$$1 \times 0 = 0$$
$$1 \times 1 = 1$$

This highlights the fact that, in binary multiplication, all one really does is perform multiplications of 1 by 1. The technique is comparable to multiplying a decimal number by a power of ten (10, 100, 1000, and so forth). The multiplicand is written down with the requisite number of zeros after it, as indicated in the example by the commas.

Example:

Decimal: 1306 × 111

```
    1 3 0 6
   ×1 1 1
   1 3 0 6,0 0
     1 3 0 6,0
       1 3 0 6
   1 4 4 9 6 6
```

Binary: (26 × 13)

```
      1 1 0 1 0
     ×1 1 0 1
     1 1 0 1 0,0 0 0
       1 1 0 1 0,0 0
       (0 0 0 0 0,0)
             1 1 0 1 0
   1 0 1 0 1 0 0 1 0  (i.e., 338)
```

Division. The basic possibilities are:

$$0 \div 1 = 0$$
$$1 \div 1 = 1$$

(Division by 0 is not possible)

Again the traditional method may be employed, working out the long division from left to right, and, as in multiplication, there is no laborious calculation of "how many times" a number will go into another number;

the divisor will divide into any part of the dividend either 1 or 0 times. In the example, commas separate the successive remainders from the next digits in the division sequence.

Example: 1101110 ÷ 101   (110 ÷ 5)
```
              0 0 1 0 1 1 0      (i.e., 22)
        101)1 1 0 1 1 1 0
            1 0 1
            0 0 1,1 1
                1 0 1
                0 1 0,1
                  1 0 1
                  0 0 0,0
```

At the end, any number less than the divisor will, of course, be a remainder, expressed in binary notation.

Binary Coding

Quite clearly, binary notation is colossally inefficient as a counting system for normal purposes. For example, to read "32" entails counting the positions of six digits—"100000"—rather than the customary two, and this ratio of approximately three digits to one is always apparent in comparing a binary number to its decimal equivalent.

At this stage, it is appropriate to examine how the computer actually uses binary notation. How it represents numbers in this way is not difficult to see, but what of letters, symbols, punctuation marks, points on a graph, image displays, and the like? First, there is a distinction to be made between the *analog computer* and the *digital computer*. The first operates by directly representing changes in one phenomenon by changes in another, as a thermometer registers changes in temperature by changes in the amount of mercury displayed in the stem of the thermometer. The second operates symbolically, by reducing all of its input to binary digits. This gives it immensely increased flexibility, and the general purpose digital computer is the one referred to throughout this text. Space does not permit an explanation of how each one of the above-mentioned types of input is translated into binary symbols, but much of the essential transformation can be illustrated by considering how the computer handles the letters and digits which make up most of ordinary text.

The key concept here is that of a *code*. The computer has been given a code system by which to translate any number or letter into a specific set of binary digits. Now, as Hayes and Becker have stressed, two things are necessary to a code: symbol and position.[1] That symbols are essential is intuitively obvious; the importance attached to the *positions* of those symbols is aptly demonstrated by the same authors' example of "god" and "dog." They continue:

> The basic issue in coding is the relationship between the number of possible codes [i.e., *code groupings*], the number of symbols, and the number of positions in which the symbols can occur. This relationship is simple:
>
> $$C=S^n,$$
>
> where C is the number of possible codes, S is the number of symbols, and n is the number of positions. For example, the number of possible codes given by three decimal digits is obviously $C = 10^3 = 1000$ (from 000 to 999). The number of possible two-letter words is $C = 26^2 = 676$ . . . and so on.[2]

Given, therefore, that the binary system is composed of only the two symbols "0" and "1," it is possible to calculate how many individual code groupings are needed to uniquely encode the elements in the various sets of characters, such as the ten decimal digits or the twenty-six letters of the alphabet. This is done by taking the number of those elements and determining the next higher power of two. Twenty-six is greater than 2^4 (16) but less than 2^5 (32): a two symbol code with five positions will provide thirty-two unique code combinations—enough for the roman alphabet with a few to spare. Figure 11 shows a very simple method for doing this by the assignment of the binary numerals to the letters of the alphabet in ascending order, starting with "1." (To see why this is not a workable system, one has only to ask how, in this code, one would represent the number 1.) In the same manner, a code with a minimum of six bit-positions would be necessary for encoding the thirty-six characters which comprise the alphabet and the decimal digits: the next higher power of two is 2^6, that is, 64.

Present-day computer hardware is usually designed to work either with a six- or an eight-bit code. (This is why computer tapes, which have one extra bit position for error-checking purposes, are almost always seven- or nine-track tapes.) The eight-bit code allows 256 different combinations —$2^8 = 256$—which permits characters to be allocated to spaces 0–255 before another bit position is needed. This is now the more commonly seen of the two. The 256 positions can accommodate all normal typographical characters and punctuation marks. Still, with both six- and eight-bit codes occasionally a situation arises in which more spaces are needed. To stop and create an entirely new code system with the extra capacity is obviously impractical; thus the problem is often conveniently solved by the reservation of one code grouping for a "shift key" symbol. When this is activated, its effect, as the name suggests, is that of a typewriter shift key; it allows the same set of symbols to function as a second set until it is deactivated.

In encoding decimal numbers in binary, there are two basic approaches. One can take a whole number, such as 74, and find the binary version of

	Binary	Decimal			Binary	Decimal
A	00001	1		N	01110	14
B	00010	2		O	01111	15
C	00011	3		P	10000	16
D	00100	4		Q	10001	17
E	00101	5		R	10010	18
F	00110	6		S	10011	19
G	00111	7		T	10100	20
H	01000	8		U	10101	21
I	01001	9		V	10110	22
J	01010	10		W	10111	23
K	01011	11		X	11000	24
L	01100	12		Y	11001	25
M	01101	13		Z	11010	26

Figure 11
Encoding the alphabet with a five-bit code

this number as a mathematician would write it; 1001010. For human beings, however, though probably not for computers, using very large numbers tends to become a very complex process, as an attempt to write the binary form of 74,000 will quickly illustrate. There is also the previously mentioned problem of ambiguity between letters and certain numbers in a pure binary system. Therefore, the more common method is to take each component of the decimal number and encode it separately; 7 as 0111 and 4 as 0100. Since one will never have to go beyond 9 (binary 1001), the largest digit used, this tactic enables one to work in binary groups of four. Thus, although more wasteful of digits than the "true binary" representation, which takes only the minimum necessary number, this principle of notation is the one generally in use, as it is far easier for human operators to handle.

Example:

Decimal Number: 74000
True Binary Version: 10010000100010000   (17 digits)
Binary Coded Decimal
Version: 7   4   0   0   0
            0111   0100   0000   0000   0000
(20 digits, but far simpler to calculate)

	ASCII*			EBCDIC	
0	0011	0000		1111	0000
1	0011	0001		1111	0001
2	0011	0010		1111	0010
3	0011	0011		1111	0011
4	0011	0100		1111	0100
5	0011	0101		1111	0101
6	0011	0110		1111	0110
7	0011	0111		1111	0111
8	0011	1000		1111	1000
9	0011	1001		1111	1001
A	0100	0001		1100	0001
B	0100	0010		1100	0010
C	0100	0011		1100	0011
D	0100	0100		1100	0100
E	0100	0101		1100	0101
F	0100	0110		1100	0110
G	0100	0111		1100	0111
H	0100	1000		1100	1000
	etc.			etc.	

*This 8-bit code is properly called "Expanded ASCII"

Figure 12
Examples of ASCII and EBCDIC coding

This latter method of treating numbers is, by extension, the same as that used for building words. Each item, a digit or a letter, is given a unique binary identity within the particular code system, and a number or word is constructed by putting these elements together in a string of data. A number thus treated is not strictly a binary number; rather it is a binary coded decimal number, and the original code for performing this operation was called Binary Coded Decimal (BCD). More recently, the Extended Binary Coded Decimal Interchange Code (EBCDIC), which is in general use on IBM computers, and the American Standard Code for Information Interchange (ASCII), which is now the official data interchange code of the federal government, have emerged as the predominant codes (*see* fig. 12). There are others, but the purpose here is not to list the various codes nor analyze their characteristics, but merely to give an outline of how the binary system has been adapted for use in computers.

The earliest computer programmers had to program entirely in binary, an enormously tedious process. As successive advances in computer design have been made, more and more of the communication hierarchy shown in figure 10 has been stored inside the machine, leaving the human operator able to write "32" or "AUTHOR = SMITH, M. J." just like that. Since the present generation of machines (the third) can work in time periods reaching into the billionths of a second, the delays involved in translating every character into, say, an eight-bit code and translating everything back into alphanumeric characters, are minimal.

Summary

The fundamental communications alphabet of the computer is the binary system, which utilizes only the two symbols "0" and "1." In a binary code containing eight positions (*binary* digi*ts,* or "bits"), 256 characters can be uniquely encoded, sufficient for the ten decimal digits, twenty-six letters, and all necessary punctuation. Many modern computers therefore now employ eight-bit codes, although the human operator is able to communicate with the machine in natural (or natural-like) language.

SAMPLE EXERCISES

1. Convert the following decimal numbers into binary numbers:
      (a) 100; (b) 127; (c) 128
   Answers:

   (a) $100 \div 2 = 50 + 0$ (b) $127 \div 2 = 63 + 1$
       $50 \div 2 = 25 + 0$ $63 \div 2 = 31 + 1$
       $25 \div 2 = 12 + 1$ $31 \div 2 = 15 + 1$
       $12 \div 2 = 6 + 0$ $15 \div 2 = 7 + 1$
       $6 \div 2 = 3 + 0$ $7 \div 2 = 3 + 1$
       $3 \div 2 = 1 + 1$ $3 \div 2 = 1 + 1$
       $1 \div 2 = 0 + 1$ $1 \div 2 = 0 + 1$
       i.e., 1100100   i.e., 1111111

   (c) It should not be necessary to do another division; adding 1 to the highest seven-digit binary number 1111111 must give the lowest eight-digit binary number 10000000, which is corroborated by the fact that $128 = 2^7$. As a parallel, perform the addition of 1 to decimal 999 to obtain 1000, or 10^3.

2. Convert the following decimal numbers into their binary coded decimal equivalents: (a) 100; (b) 127; (c) 128; (d) 17,246,981.
Answers:

(a) 0001 0000 0000
(b) 0001 0010 0111
(c) 0001 0010 1000
(d) 0001 0111 0010 0100 0110 1001 1000 0001

3. Ascertain, without performing the conversion, how many digits would be required to code 2(d) in binary form.
Answer: 25 (17,246,981 is greater than 2^{24} but less than 2^{25})

4. Convert the following binary numbers into decimal numbers:
(a) 111101000; (b) 111111000; (c) 1111101000
Answers:

	2^9	2^8	2^7	2^6	2^5	2^4	2^3	2^2	2	1
(a)		1	1	1	1	0	1	0	0	0
(b)		1	1	1	1	1	1	0	0	0
(c)	1	1	1	1	1	1	0	1	0	0	0

After placing the numbers under their respective powers of two, we see that (a) gives:

$$2^8 + 2^7 + 2^6 + 2^5 + 2^3 = 256 + 128 + 64 + 32 + 8 = 488$$

We also notice that the only difference between (a) and (b) is the addition of a 1 in the 2^4 column. There is thus no need to repeat the whole sum; (b) gives:

$$488 + 16 = 504$$

Furthermore, (c) is (a) with an extra digit at the front, representing 2^9 (512). Thus (c) gives:

$$488 + 512 = 1000$$

5. Assume that an average book consists of 250 pages. Each page has forty lines, and each line has ten words plus spacing and punctuation. Assume that the average word length (including punctuation and one space) for all the languages represented in the library is seven characters, and that it takes eight binary digits to encode one character.
(a) How many characters does an average-sized book contain? (700,000)
(b) How many binary digits would be necessary to represent one such book? (5,600,000)

(c) If a 2400-foot reel of computer tape can store 45 million characters, how many books could be contained on one reel of tape? (64)

(d) At this ratio of books per tape, how many reels would be necessary to store an entire library of 1.28 million books of average size? (20,000)

Assume that the average catalog record contains 500 characters, and that each of the 1.28 million books in the library needed six catalog cards (including all added entries, but ignoring subject cross-reference cards, guide cards, and the like).

(e) How many characters would the card catalog contain? (3,840,000,000)

(f) If one on-line disk storage device can hold the equivalent of one reel of tape, 45 million characters, how many such devices would be needed to put the entire card catalog of this library on-line? (86)

Notes

1. Robert M. Hayes and Joseph Becker, *Handbook of Data Processing for Libraries* (New York: Wiley, 1970), p. 220.
2. Ibid.

6

Boolean
Logic and
Weighting

Introduction

In preceding chapters the characteristics of a *typical* bibliographic reference file of computer-readable data have been examined, and the special-purpose list of subject terms, the thesaurus around which such a file is built, has been explored. The following two chapters are concerned with how a search is accomplished. It is worth stating, at the outset, that in constructing a search which needs a computer to carry it out, librarians are doing essentially what they have always done: acting as a mediator (an "interface") between the patron on the one hand, and on the other, a body of knowledge organized for the express purpose of facilitating its retrieval. A vital part of the librarian's responsibility has always been to mediate an intellectual organization of knowledge to the user—to explain, when someone asks for material on "Performing Arts," that this will be found under "Theater Arts" (and sometimes to explain why); obviously this should continue to be true regardless of which particular storage medium happens to contain the information. Furthermore, in doing a computerized bibliographic search, all the librarian's insights into, and experience with, such matters as correct bibliographic references, the terminology of subject control, and the world of print-publishing are invaluable assets, just as they are in conventional bibliographic searching. The difference is that now the process of searching becomes a formalized sequence of steps which serve to give the computer the detailed and precise instructions it must have in order to function. Therefore, in some situations more thought has to be devoted to the logic of what needs to be done—implicit as well as explicit. The consequences of this will be discussed after the basic tool of search formulation, Boolean logic, is outlined.

Boolean Logic

As noted, the process of answering a patron's request via a computer consists of a formalized sequence of steps. First the request is expressed as an ordinary *natural-language statement* (unlike much across-the-desk reference work, this statement *must* be written down by either the patron or the librarian). Next, the statement is examined by the librarian, analyzed, and recast as a *logical formula* suitable for processing by the computer.

In the majority of bibliographic searches, a subject approach is called for, though obviously sometimes certain authors may have been specified for inclusion or exclusion, and, just as obviously, there may be other boundary conditions (parameters), such as the date or language of publication. Analysis of the subject content will normally mean consulting a thesaurus, which is, as previously noted, somewhat similar to a subject heading list. The result of this phase of the process will customarily be the selection of a list of terms which will fully and accurately cover the request. The next stage is the combining of these terms in a way which will elicit the best results from the computer, and at this time there are two principal methods of linking the terms: *Boolean algebra* and *Weighting*. At present the first is more widely utilized, but the two may be used in combination. Note that the choice of one or both of these methods is embodied in the programs that are employed to search the data base, and has nothing inherently to do with the data base, the records that comprise it, or the computer's own internal operating system.

First developed and codified by the English mathematician George Boole (1815–1864), Boolean logic is a technique of using the most basic conceivable forms of expression to represent any logical possibility: that is, a thing either exists or does not exist, is either present or not present, operative or not operative, and so on. It is used in the present context to turn natural language requests into an unambiguous, highly specific format for manipulation by the computer. As indicated in chapter 5, this "yes-or-no" mode is at the heart of all computer operations: for example, a switch is either *on* or *off;* current is either flowing or not; and it is by having the computer make that binary choice at every available character space on the magnetic medium, that data is encoded and later read. Because his new method of logical analysis freed philosophy from many an impasse and opened up entire new vistas of thought (not the least important of which is its recent applicability to computer searches), Boole is regarded as a seminal influence in modern symbolic logic.[1]

The following explanation of how Boolean logic is used makes no claim to be either mathematically sophisticated or logically exhaustive. It is a basic outline, written by librarians for other librarians, representing the foundation of what librarians who help patrons with computer searches should know about how this form of information retrieval is accomplished. For those desiring a more detailed exposition, there are a number of authoritative and well-written texts.[2]

Strictly speaking, Boolean logic provides two conditions to express the relationships between elements of data; in practice, this is extended to three by the use of negative logic. The three conditions are *AND, OR,* and *NOT* (which is the logical opposite of *AND,* and is sometimes written as *AND NOT).*

1. The use of *AND* (A *AND* B) means that *both* elements must occur before the document is retrieved. This is known as the *intersection* of A and B.

2. The use of *OR* (A *OR* B) means that the user is interested in those documents containing A, and those documents containing B. This is the *union* of A and B. Note that this use of the word "and" is different from logical *AND*—it is, in effect, what is meant in ordinary language by that most convenient expression "and/or," as in "We will travel by ship and/or plane." The three possibilities, then, are either ship or plane or both. *OR* is inclusive, while *AND* is exclusive. Note that the two tend to pull the search results in opposite directions (too broad or too narrow) and must therefore be used in a judicious balance. The logical term *OR* employed in this sense is often referred to as the "inclusive disjunction"; that is, the disjunction of the two elements is required (A *OR* B) but so is their inter-section (A *AND* B). This is the prevailing usage of logical *OR,* but the reader should be aware that it can also designate an "exclusive disjunction," where the disjunction (A *OR* B) is required, but the intersection of the terms is specifically excluded; the complete expression would then read: A *OR* B *AND NOT* (A *AND* B). For information retrieval applications, the latter mode is rarely used; this will become clearer when the manipula-tion of actual subject terms in Boolean fashion is discussed.

3. The use of *NOT* (A *NOT* B) implies *AND NOT,* as previously noted. There is virtually no significance, as common sense will confirm, to

a request for A *OR NOT* B, for everything which contained A and every-thing not containing B would be retrieved; this would almost certainly pro-duce an unusably large segment of the file. It is crucial to remember that in many programming systems, *NOT*-logic takes precedence in a search over the other modes; that is to say, where no priorities are given, an operating sequence is established by the computer in order to avoid am-biguity. Typically, this order of importance is *NOT, AND,* then *OR.* If one gives the computer a *NOT* term it usually tests for the existence of that term first. Only if it does not find that term does the computer bother working through the successive Boolean relationships to see if the rest of the logic matches. Figure 13 presents the three Boolean connectors with their notations and meaning.

Boolean Connectors	Symbols	Examples	Meanings
AND	. &	A · B A & B	Both A and B must be true or must occur
OR	+ ǀ	A + B A ǀ B	Either A or B must be true or must occur
NOT	– ¬	A · $\overline{B}$ A &¬B (A¬B)	A must be true or must occur and B must be not true or must not occur

Figure 13
Boolean connectors

Note that in figure 13 two symbols are given for each connector; the first is the traditional arithmetic notation, while the second shows the con-ventional typographical symbols that have been developed for use on key-boards to input data to the computer via card punches, video terminals, magnetic tape typewriters, and the like. The vertical line representing *OR* is sometimes known as Sheffer's stroke. In using these symbols, one must remember that "+" equals logical *OR,* not logical *AND.*

Venn Diagrams

Another way of representing these relationships is by the use of Venn diagrams, named after John Venn (1834–1923), the English logician. By inventing them Venn produced, as Martin Gardner says, "a diagrammatic method so perfectly isomorphic with the Boolean class algebra, and picturing the structure of class logic with such visual clarity, that even a non-mathematically minded philosopher could 'see' what the new logic was all about."[3]

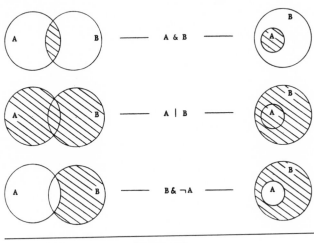

Figure 14
Venn diagrams

Venn diagrams are becoming a familiar and graphic way of sorting out the simple logical relationships between objects or classes of objects. For obvious reasons, they are not recommended for portraying interrelationships between more than three members. They can be quickly and conveniently employed if it appears that they will clarify the real nature of a search; they may also aid the patron in defining his needs more accurately. If, on the other hand, they do not appear to be of any particular value, this step is not obligatory—it is merely a convenience. One fact, which figure 14 makes clear, is that there is more than one possible way to characterize a search statement such as A *AND* B; A might be a complete subset of B, which is properly known as the *inclusion* of A in B.[4]

Parentheses

Groups of terms may be combined by the use of parentheses to make more complex logical formulations. Usually these will be terms with some degree of affinity, such as synonyms. Again, the ability to do this in a search is a function of whatever programs are being used to process the file, not of the file or data themselves. It is conceivable that the organizing capability furnished by parentheses might not be included in the question-building devices of a system, but in practice this would prove so restrictive that the use of parentheses is generally taken for granted. Even when the syntactical conventions of the particular program do not actually allow parentheses as such, the hierarchical effect of parenthetic logic is usually achieved in some other fashion.

All formulations employing at least one such grouping of terms need parentheses in order to be expressed unambiguously:

$$(A \mid B) \quad \& \quad (C \mid D)$$

Furthermore, computers can manipulate with the greatest of ease expressions containing multiple parentheses *nested* one within the other:

$$((A \mid B) \quad \& \quad (C \mid D)) \quad \& \quad (X \mid Y)$$

Note that the only viable way to build such expressions is by starting at the core and working out, adding parentheses as one finishes identifying first a small subgroup of terms, then a larger group, and so on:

1. $(A \mid B) \quad \& \quad (C \mid D)$
2. $((A \mid B) \quad \& \quad (C \mid D)) \quad \& \quad (X \mid Y)$

this could continue with further analysis of term D:

3. $((A \mid B) \quad \& \quad (C \mid D \mid (D_1 \mid D_2 \mid D_3))) \quad \& \quad ((V \mid W) \quad \& \quad (X \mid Y))$

As may be seen underneath all the parentheses, line 3 of the above illustration is a simple A & B type of request, pivoted by the second "&" sign (indicated by an arrow), in which both terms have been subdivided for greater breadth or depth of coverage.

Computers handle parentheses by what is essentially a counting technique, matching the number of left parentheses against the number of right parentheses. Since counting is something that present-day computers can do several million times faster than any human, it is not infeasible for search programs to allow fifteen or twenty levels of parentheses. The only practical limit is set by the human's ability to conceive of an information need possessing that order of sophistication.

Note that one can be logical and redundant at the same time by asking for the same thing more than once:

$$A \mid (A \ \& \ B)$$

anything containing A & B must, ipso facto, be included in the class of objects which contains merely A.

For most normal searching operations, however, it is seldom necessary to go beyond one level of nesting, that is, the use of double parentheses. In most situations it is reasonable to assume that anything more involuted than that will be so logically restrictive as to retrieve almost nothing at all. At this point another factor becomes crucial, namely the size of the file. Obviously, the more references the computer is asked to scan, the more of a chance it will have of finding at least one entry that meets the criteria. The *Research in Education* file contains, as of this writing, about 70,000 citations; the MARC file is already well over 200,000; the total MEDLARS data base has approximately 1.5 million. In ten years, none of these figures will seem especially large.

Weighting

The term "weighting" has been used in two related senses in information storage and retrieval. Its original meaning was that of an indexing technique of assigning numerical values to the index terms, so as to indicate their relative importance in the document being indexed. This was reckoned to be a significant advance in the state of the art of indexing, in that it allowed a much more sophisticated approach for search and retrieval; it arose at the time of the first experiments investigating the possibilities for automatic content analysis by computer. It was hoped that cheap (in terms of machine time) and reliable methods could be devised, methods by which the computer could perform the assignment of weights to the key terms selected according to various statistical or semantic tests of the full text or, more frequently, of the abstract. However, that hope has not yet been realized, and insofar as term weights must be assigned by a human indexer, the time taken to index a document rises so steeply that it becomes prohibitive. Therefore, very few existing files of machine-readable data possess fully developed weighting of subject terms as a regular feature of the record (if the institution acquiring the file wishes to add them, it can, of course, do so, subject to copyright and to the heavy cost of reprocessing). Some files provide a broad division of the assigned terms into two or three ranks of relative importance; the ERIC indexing process, as previously noted, uses an asterisk for the major descriptors, thus giving a two-fold ranking.

Out of this ingenious, though as yet imperfectly realized, concept, the idea of using numerical weights in the retrieval process was developed. It was quickly perceived that this could be done *whether or not* the references to be searched possessed weighted subject access. Its effect is to permit some shading in a request—something more flexible than the rigid Boolean categories will allow—and thus it is probably employed to best advantage in conjunction with a Boolean approach, rather than instead of it. Again it should be stressed that this mode of searching is a capability of the particular search program(s) being used, not of the computer nor, in most instances, of the record format itself.

Weighting of a search request, which is the only concern here, consists of attaching a numerical value to the search terms in the order of their importance, and then specifying a *threshold weight,* or *threshold value.* In performing the search, the computer is made to add the terms in the bibliographic entry according to the given table of weights, and to retrieve only those whose total weight equals or exceeds the threshold, any assigned terms for which no weight has been specified naturally having a value of zero. A single, fairly straightforward example will illustrate. If a patron requested material on "the teaching of American History to minority children in primary grades, especially in large city school systems, preferably written after 1965," the librarian might elect to search the ERIC files for the following:

ERIC Descriptor	Weight
AMERICAN HISTORY	20
PRIMARY GRADES	20
MINORITY GROUP CHILDREN	6
MEXICAN AMERICANS	5
NEGROES	5
AMERICAN INDIANS	3
URBAN SCHOOLS	2
(Date equal to or greater than 1966)	1
THRESHOLD WEIGHT: 46	

To achieve the threshold of 46, only certain combinations of the elements of the search (which in this example are subject terms and a date, though clearly the technique can be applied to any searchable data element) would produce a match, or "hit." Occurrence of the three most significant terms will cause a hit; material about the teaching of American History to either of the ethnic groups weighted with "5" will be retrieved if it also concerns urban schools *or* was written after 1965; a document solely about American Indian children must have both those qualifications, or must be a comparative study involving at least one other minority group, and so on.

Weighting thus represents a means of responding to the individual nuances and emphases which the patron places on his request, expressed in this example by the words "especially" and "preferably." This is exactly the way in which many reference inquiries are framed, and the shading is often a critical aspect of the question. If Boolean expressions allow for the definition in detail of elements wanted and not wanted, weights allow the introduction of a scale of *how much* a particular element is wanted or not wanted. In this illustration, the implication is that material on American Indian children is not desired *unless* it has at least one further term of interest; implicit also is the fact that although pre-1965 literature is generally not of interest, the patron is not excluding it if other considerations put the document squarely in his field of interest.

Arithmetic Operators

In the example on weighting, a further refinement was introduced into the search specifications: "Date equal to or greater than 1966." This is an arithmetic command; it instructs the computer to carry out a simple arithmetic test in order to accomplish that part of the search. Like the weighting of terms, this technique enables the requester to expand upon the plain Boolean categories by specifying a *range* of values for a particular item in the record. It will be obvious that for the arithmetic approach to have any advantage, the system must be able to perform at least the three basic comparisons Equal To, Greater Than, and Less Than. In practice, this is usually increased to the five choices shown below, with their standard abbreviations and arithmetic symbols.

Arithmetic Operation	*Abbreviation*	*Symbol*
EQUAL TO	EQ	=
GREATER THAN	GT	>
LESS THAN	LT	<
GREATER THAN OR EQUAL TO	GE	≥
LESS THAN OR EQUAL TO	LE	≤

Having received an arithmetic operator, the computer can then be left to test for all the possibilities for a match, which it will do by a simple comparison of the two numbers. Obviously, the larger a range of numerals that can be compared automatically, the more profitable it is for the human operator to avoid doing it; thus the technique can be especially fruitful in a retrospective search of several years of material. It should also be noted that, search programs permitting, it is possible to superimpose a Boolean operation onto the arithmetic one:

$$DATE > 1959 \quad AND < 1970$$

would retrieve anything published during the decade of the 1960s, as would

$$DATE \geq 1960 \quad AND \leq 1969$$

Arithmetic operators can also accommodate exclusion of values or ranges of value,

$$AND \ NOT \ (DATE = 1960)$$

To exclude a range of values, it is merely necessary to formulate the statement in the logically opposite way to that which one would use to include that range. Requesting

$$DATE \ NOT \ (> 1960)$$

is identically expressed without the use of NOT by

$$DATE \ (\leq 1960)$$

As will be readily observed, this capability, exploited in coordination with Boolean logic and the use of weights on such fields as "Author" and "Descriptors," would provide an extremely flexible and sophisticated search. At this date, however, it appears to be true that most search systems do not extend that far. As mentioned elsewhere in this chapter, the sheer size of the files that are becoming available for a machine search (*Chemical Abstracts* alone is now issuing over a million new citations every three years) will compel the development of finer and finer screens with which to sift the relevant information from the ever-increasing quantities that will be irrelevant.

Summary

Computerized searching of bibliographic data bases involves turning a natural language statement into an explicitly logical formula, using the Boolean connectors *AND, OR,* and *NOT. AND*-logic is exclusive, whereas *OR*-logic is inclusive. These logical relationships can often be clarified by the use of Venn diagrams. A further technique, which permits the introduction of some "shading" into a request, is *weighting,* whereby numerical weights are assigned to search terms according to their degree of importance. Arithmetic operators (Equal To, Greater Than, Less Than, and so on) can be employed to search numerical parts of the record.

SAMPLE EXERCISES

1. A | B & C | D   is an ambiguous formulation. Using the hierarchy of logical operations discussed earlier, place parentheses around it to show how the machine would interpret it, then restructure it according to this hierarchy.

Answer: A | (B & C) | D which becomes (B & C) | A | D

2. A | B & C ¬D   is an ambiguous formulation. Proceed as in (1).

Answer: (A | (B & C)) ¬D which becomes ¬D & ((B & C) | A)

3. (A | B) & (C | D)   is a valid compound formulation, which can be expanded into a series of simple disjunctions (*AND*-statements linked by *OR*) until all the possible combinations that would fit this formulation have been exhausted. How many such simple statements are there, and what are they?

Answer:

(A & C) | (A & D) | (B & C) | (B & D) |
(A & B & C) | (A & B & D) | (A & C & D) |
                                      (B & C & D) |
(A & B & C & D)

a total of nine. (Note: this series is the logical string which more closely represents how the computer actually searches.)

Notes

1. See, for example, M. Cohen and E. Nagel, *An Introduction to Logic and Scientific Method* (New York: Harcourt, 1934), p. 112.
2. John G. Kemeny, J. Laurie Snell, and Gerald L. Thompson, *Introduction to Finite Mathematics,* 2d ed. (Englewood Cliffs, N.J.: Prentice-Hall, 1966); D. Kalish and R. Montague, *Logic: Techniques of Formal Reasoning* (New York: Harcourt, 1964); and Gerald J. Massey, *Understanding Symbolic Logic* (New York: Harper, 1970).

3. Martin Gardner, *Logic Machines and Diagrams* (New York: McGraw-Hill, 1958), p. 39.
4. Two texts which are particularly useful in explaining Venn diagrams are: Irving M. Copi, *Introduction to Logic,* 3d ed. (New York: Macmillan, 1968), chaps. 5 and 6; and Morris Kline, *Mathematics for Liberal Arts* (Reading, Mass.: Addison-Wesley, 1967), p. 491–98. The latter develops an example based on libraries.

7

Search
Strategies

Many feasible strategies have been developed for the extracting of information from the different categories of machine-readable data bases. *Weighting* has already been mentioned as a useful complement to the strictly Boolean approach in processing bibliographic files; another method often used on textual material is a *string search,* in which the computer simply scans the file for a direct match with a given string of characters. This method allows bypassing many of the complexities of subject indexing, but possesses the drawbacks implicit in asking the computer to search only for the specific string of data enclosed between quotes or some other delimiter: thus "MACHINE READABLE" would miss "MACHINE-READABLE"; "JONES P. J." would miss "JONES PJ" and all the other possible versions of that author's name. For these reasons, string searching on subject words is more suited to full-text files than to bibliographic ones. For example, full-text files of legal information, such as U.S. state constitutions and statutes, are now available in machine-readable form: when the computer is given a key legal phrase, such as "search and seizure" or "grievous bodily harm," it will display, in context, successive appearances of that phrase. This is not intended to imply that the string search is the only, or even necessarily the most efficient, way to approach this type of file, but it does avoid complexity and is sometimes adequate. The basic rule for such a search is that there should be no possibility for ambiguity as to the form in which a particular item of data appears in the record. Other data elements which meet this test are: journal *coden,* numbered subsections of a file, the first few characters of a classification number, and various codes for language and country of publication. Here, too, a string search can be effective as a filtering or screening mechanism, used before proceeding to a finer search.

Numerical files, of course, give rise to an entirely different set of processing options involving statistical analysis and computation to derive what is actually new data. These cannot be covered in the present work. However, Boolean strategy has wide applicability to bibliographic file searching and is the technique most commonly in use at present. It should be apparent from the previous chapter that the Boolean connectors *AND, OR,* and *NOT* constitute a potentially powerful and sophisticated technique of machine-oriented subject searching.

Although the reader should obviously expect to encounter variations, depending upon his locale and the search system available, the *basic steps* involved in running a computer search may be identified as follows:

1. Obtain a statement of interest from the user.
2. Analyze the statement of interest in terms of its major concepts.
3. Formulate a machine-readable query (often known as a profile).
4. Run the formulated query.
5. Examine the results.
6. If necessary, modify the query and resubmit it.

This chapter is concerned with steps 1 to 3, namely, the basic procedures for procurement and analysis of the request and formulation of the query which corresponds to it. The next chapter deals with steps 4 to 6.

The *statement of interest* is, broadly speaking, designed to elicit the patron's response to the question, "On what subject (or area, or topic) do you desire information?" Again, this *must* be expressed as a written statement, for reasons which will become increasingly clear. As a rule, those who are responsible for formulating and running searches will wish to employ a form which leads the user to provide this information in a way that the system can utilize. Therefore, although the heart of such a form should be a prose description by the patron of his area of interest, it is frequently useful to provide space for the listing of specific subject terms; crucial authors, institutions, or projects having a bearing on the topic; language restrictions; and the like. Any information identified at this early stage which will assist the search analyst and otherwise help to ensure a successful search will, of course, save added time and effort, not to mention frustration, later on. Any instructions given to the patron should therefore include such a phrase as, "Be as detailed and specific as you can."

Because the reader of this text will probably be among those eventually called upon to take responsibility for the analysis of requests prior to a machine search, a fairly typical statement of interest form has been reproduced in Appendix C. This statement is merely one to which the authors had ready access and should not be treated as the last word. Many comparable forms already exist—the MEDLARS system, quite naturally, being one of the first to use an extended, multipart form—but if, in his own environment, the reader feels circumstances demand that he design one of his own, he should do so without hesitation.

Next, someone with the requisite subject competence, preferably a librarian, since a librarian is likely also to have bibliographic expertise and information handling experience, should analyze the "raw" request in terms of its major concepts, or broad areas of interest, whether openly stated in the question or not. Since the two or three main concepts within a question are ultimately to be joined together by *AND*-logic—A & B & C— the intent here is to determine the essentials. What are the areas of interest or aspects of coverage which, if lacking, would cause the citation to be rejected, even though it may contain *some* degree of significance? In the above example, the presence of A and B, which logically represents two-thirds of the area of interest, is unimportant unless C is also found. Examples of suitable candidates for the status of major concepts are: in chemistry, an element or compound, a reaction or process, an effect or phenomenon; in biology, an organ, a disease, a drug; in engineering, a material, a technique or process, an instrument or machine, a structure; in education, a grouping by such factors as age, ethnic origin, geographic area, intelligence level, an academic subject, a teaching technique, a psychological factor. The aim is to answer the familiar question, "What is this request really about?"

Using the thesaurus, where one exists, one should next analyze each main grouping, since it is very probable that more than one term will be called for in order to define adequately these broad concepts. The ERIC *Thesaurus* is typical, in that it allows for the selection of *broader, narrower,* and otherwise *related* terms. All the terms within one grouping, or parameter,* will generally be linked by *OR*-logic, which, as mentioned above, can be taken to be *inclusive* in function, whereas *AND*-logic is *exclusive*.

---

* This term was brought into general use in this sense by Chemical Abstracts Service.

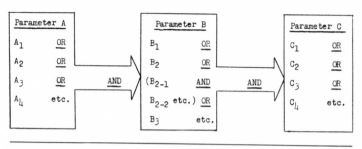

Figure 15
Logical representation of a typical search

By a judicious blend of the two, it is possible to build questions which are substantial enough to produce much relevant material, and sophisticated enough to take full advantage of the computer's incredible capacity for meticulously detailed and accurate searching. A typical search request may thus be diagrammed as in figure 15.

The minimum criterion for retrieval of a citation under these conditions is one term from each parameter, but obviously an item possessing more than this would also be a hit—presumably a progressively more relevant one.

As will become apparent, there are practical limitations on how many groupings to erect, and the number of terms to include in them. Between two and four parameters, each containing between three and six terms, will probably garner the best results in most of the searches typically met, depending upon the size of the file and the frequency of the terms.

Notice that, within this basic framework of employing *OR*-logic inside parameters and *AND*-logic to link parameters together, certain variations are possible: in figure 15 we have used *AND* in parameter B in a perfectly valid way to distinguish between two levels in the subject hierarchy— either we want B_2 or we must have all of its subdivisions. (If this were a geographic locator, for example, we might want either GREAT BRITAIN *OR* SCOTLAND *AND* WALES *AND* ENGLAND *AND* NORTHERN IRELAND). Most search systems are designed to permit several levels of logic; *AND* is usually implied between the major concepts, but it is sometimes not permitted within a parameter, which is then by definition restricted to *OR*-logic. In such systems, any terms which are to be connected by logical *AND* must form a new parameter. The librarian or search analyst must naturally learn these elementary logical capabilities of the system before constructing the first search.

The following example is designed to illustrate the basic steps in the analysis of a statement of interest and its formulation into a profile:

Statement of Interest:

"I am looking for material on the use of innovative teaching tools (for example, audiovisuals) in nonpublic schools, particularly in the smaller schools, such as church schools."

First attempt:

Parameter A	AND	Parameter B	
INSTRUCTIONAL AIDS	OR	CATHOLIC SCHOOLS	OR
INSTRUCTIONAL MATERIALS	OR	CATHOLIC ELEMENTARY	
INSTRUCTIONAL MEDIA		SCHOOLS	OR
		PRIVATE SCHOOLS	

An evaluation shows that the first parameter is obviously too vague and general. A further search through the *Thesaurus* might produce the following:

Second attempt:

Parameter A	AND	Parameter B	
INSTRUCTIONAL AIDS	OR	CATHOLIC SCHOOLS	OR
INSTRUCTIONAL INNOVATION	OR	CATHOLIC ELEMENTARY	
INSTRUCTIONAL MEDIA	OR	SCHOOLS	OR
INSTRUCTIONAL TELEVISION	OR	PAROCHIAL SCHOOLS	OR
TEACHING MACHINES		PRIVATE SCHOOLS	OR
		PROPRIETARY SCHOOLS	

This formulation is clearly an improvement but still could produce marginally relevant hits (such as, "INSTRUCTIONAL AIDS" in "PRIVATE SCHOOLS," where the aids are traditional aids, not innovative ones, and the schools are not church schools). At this point, further analysis reveals that the broad conceptual area of *innovation* could be separated from the broad conceptual area of *instructional aids:*

Third attempt:

Parameter A	AND	Parameter B	AND	Parameter C	
INSTRUCTIONAL AIDS	OR	INSTRUCTIONAL INNOVATION	OR	CATHOLIC SCHOOLS	OR
INSTRUCTIONAL MATERIALS	OR	INNOVATION	OR	CATHOLIC ELEMENTARY SCHOOLS	OR
INSTRUCTIONAL MEDIA	OR	EDUCATIONAL INNOVATION		PAROCHIAL SCHOOLS	OR
INSTRUCTIONAL TELEVISION	OR			PRIVATE SCHOOLS	OR
TEACHING MACHINES				PROPRIETARY SCHOOLS	

The foregoing example points up the element of choice in the construction of a computerized search. As is true in other facets of complex library reference work, there will almost always be several equally valid approaches to a problem. In formulating computer searches, this means grouping the main concepts and selecting the appropriate family of terms for each one. These are the tasks in which librarians, more than any other professional group, can be of most help to the patron. Apart from the exercise of judgment about the best subject terms, the librarians' responsibility is to utilize their understanding of the information transfer process itself; this means that they should develop a feeling for the underlying dynamics of the searching process. Unquestionably, the major source of this practical skill is the regular performance of searches and careful analysis of results; but a few pointers may be given here.

1. AND-*logic*. It is possible, and, in certain circumstances appropriate, to construct parameters containing only one term each. In general, however, this is to be avoided. Joining three individual subject terms with *AND*-logic, A & B & C, is tantamount to claiming that these terms alone are sufficient to retrieve the *total* number of relevant references in the file, and that the hierarchical or other relational structure of the thesaurus has no value. Given a system such as ERIC, which customarily indexes documents with anything from ten to twenty terms, this is unlikely in practice, and in fact bears out the librarian's day-by-day experience in the use of subject heading systems, that a single term is frequently not enough. In addition, not all descriptors occur with comparable frequency. This is a reality to be remembered continually, although one is particularly susceptible to its effects if one elects to work in one-term parameters. Figure 16 illustrates what could happen in such circumstances. One valid way in which this approach might be used is in retrieving a citation which is known to be in the file. For example, to obtain a better quality printout of figure 20 in chapter 8, the authors ran the search again, searching only for "ENGLISH (SECOND LANGUAGE)" *AND* "PARAGRAPH COMPOSITION," on the assumption that only one entry would contain this intersection of terms in a quarterly segment of the file. However, this is a somewhat specialized use of the file, which does not detract from the relevance of the general procedure for "real" searches.

As was noted earlier, the basic working rule should be: "try to express the question in approximately three broad conceptual areas." However, in dealing with a small segment of data, such as the current portion of a serial bibliographic file (containing 3,000–5,000 citations) only a two-parameter search may be fruitful. Conversely, a request to scan something like 500,000 or one million records can be somewhat more complicated

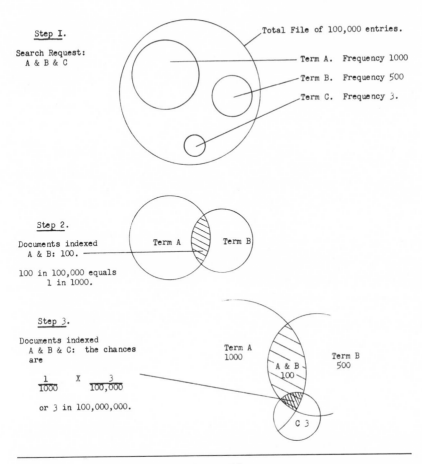

Step 1.

Search Request:
A & B & C

Total File of 100,000 entries.

Term A. Frequency 1000

Term B. Frequency 500

Term C. Frequency 3.

Step 2.

Documents indexed
A & B: 100.

100 in 100,000 equals
1 in 1000.

Term A   Term B

Step 3.

Documents indexed
A & B & C: the chances
are

$$\frac{1}{1000} \quad X \quad \frac{3}{100,000}$$

or 3 in 100,000,000.

Term A
1000

A & B
100

Term B
500

C 3

Figure 16
Importance of descriptor frequency statistics

(requiring, say, four well-developed parameters) and still produce a substantial output. Obviously it is not only the size of the file, but also the
amount of indexing done per document, which affects the number of parameters it is sensible to use. Asking for the co-occurrence of four or more
terms out of twenty means the chances of retrieving anything are incredibly
small. If documents were indexed with 100 descriptors, a ten-parameter
search would not be outrageous; at present, with a pragmatic limit of about
twenty terms per document in most systems, it certainly would be.

2. OR-*logic.* The converse of the above line of thought is clear—overuse
of *OR*-logic can result in too broad a coverage. A one-parameter search,
especially if subdivided (A|B|C|D|E), is obviously too broad for most
people's needs. Even a two- or three-parameter search can produce "gar-

bage" if each of the parameters contains a long *OR*-logic string of high-frequency descriptors, or if the term groupings have not been sensitively arranged. To give a simple example, let us assume that a researcher wants material on teaching reading to retarded children with the aid of teaching machines. Then, "READING INSTRUCTION" & "(RETARDED CHILDREN|TEACHING MACHINES)" will obviously produce hits on the teaching of reading with the aid of teaching machines. This should have been a legitimate three-parameter search. Although three single descriptors are given here to simplify the example, the same is obviously true where the terms have been developed into parameters. One unrelated term in an otherwise homogenous grouping can destroy the intended logic in this fashion, producing what is known as a "false coordination" or "false drop." A good rule of thumb is to employ *OR*-logic mainly for synonyms, near synonyms, and word variants.

3. *Descriptor Frequency.* In most automated bibliographic information storage and retrieval systems—as in most manual ones—the subject terms display an enormous variation in the frequency with which they occur. This can hinder retrieval efforts in a number of ways if it is not allowed for. If descriptors are mismatched, situations such as that illustrated by figure 16 can occur. Again, by extension, this applies to multiterm parameters, with the same effect. However, as a corollary, remember that these "broad" or "general" terms with extremely high frequency (terms that searchers, in their striving for pinpoint accuracy, often like to ignore) do have their value. To reiterate, indexing is done simply and solely to facilitate retrieval, to provide the eventual users with better prospects of access to the information they need. It follows that indexers are always trying to anticipate what the users' reactions will be, and if the ERIC indexers, over a period of years, have used "INSTRUCTIONAL MATERIALS" more than 3,400 times (over 5.5 percent of the entire ERIC RIE file as of December 1971) it is plain that this is one of the central topics of coverage in the ERIC system, that the indexer expects many users to need it, and that this descriptor should be examined. By incorporating such a term into a search with other, less frequently used descriptors, it is possible to employ it as a first, coarse filter.

The full potential of descriptor frequency statistics as an aid to efficiency in searching has not yet been exploited, largely because so few systems have made them available as yet. This is certain to change as computerized searching becomes more and more widespread, and as the multimillion record file becomes commonplace. Some systems publish statistics on descriptor frequencies: these are always most valuable and should be obtained, when available, for any data base being processed. These statistics generally appear in one or more of the following ways:

Postings List: an alphabetical list of descriptors, with the identification numbers of documents using the descriptor posted against it (*see* fig. 17). This is often known as an *inverted file,* and by next searching for the citations corresponding to the list of numbers appearing under a given term, a first, broad search at very little machine cost can be achieved. Against these savings, however, must be weighed the cost of creating the file.

Frequency Alphabetic List: an alphabetical list of descriptors, showing the current frequency number for each entry (*see* fig. 18).

Frequency List by Frequency: the list of descriptors, sorted in descending order of frequency, and then alphabetically within frequency (*see* fig. 19).

Whenever such listings are available, it is often a good idea to keep them at the reference desk, readily accessible to patrons as well as li-

FREQ	DESCRIPTOR				
1	ABILITY				
	ED027883				
1	ABILITY GROUPING				
	ED027009				
4	ABILITY IDENTIFICATION				
	ED012166	ED012612	ED012613	ED013103	
3	ABLE STUDENTS				
	ED012580	ED014308	ED019076		
1	ABSTRACT REASONING				
	ED024325				
1	ABSTRACTS				
	ED013607				
19	ACADEMIC ABILITY				
	ED010098	ED010954	ED011190	ED011191	ED011771
	ED011778	ED012157	ED012181	ED012609	ED013082
	ED013106	ED014277	ED020728	ED021539	ED022436
	ED022454	ED024354	ED025264	ED027016	

Figure 17
Descriptor postings list:
ERIC-RIE junior college subset

FREQ	DESCRIPTOR
1	ABILITY
1	ABILITY GROUPING
4	ABILITY IDENTIFICATION
2	ABLE STUDENTS
1	ABSTRACT REASONING
1	ABSTRACTS
19	ACADEMIC ABILITY
52	ACADEMIC ACHIEVEMENT
7	ACADEMIC APTITUDE
5	ACADEMIC ASPIRATION
5	ACADEMIC EDUCATION
2	ACADEMIC ENRICHMENT
1	ACADEMIC FAILURE
3	ACADEMIC FREEDOM
34	ACADEMIC PERFORMANCE
15	ACADEMIC PROBATION
5	ACADEMIC RANK (PROFESSIONAL)
1	ACADEMIC RECORDS
6	ACADEMIC STANDARDS
2	ACCELERATED PROGRAMS

Figure 18
Frequency alphabetic descriptor list:
ERIC-RIE junior college subset

brarians. Most library users tend to be unaware of the existence of such statistics, and will be fascinated to have their significance for searching explained.

It is anticipated that a "hit prediction" program will increasingly form part of a search system, and become a routine element in the performance of a search. Already it is becoming commonplace in interactive search systems for the user to sit at a terminal and enter a request, and for the computer then to scan the inverted file and reply with a message such as, "The file contains 728 items which fulfill this request. Do you wish to narrow the search?" A mathematical hit prediction routine, which could be run in the computer's central processing unit without any need for storage of even an inverted file, would be much cheaper. By typing in the logical expression of a search, the frequency count for each descriptor

FREQ	DESCRIPTOR
1200	JUNIOR COLLEGES
146	VOCATIONAL EDUCATION
131	TECHNICAL EDUCATION
130	HIGHER EDUCATION
111	QUESTIONNAIRES
111	STUDENT CHARACTERISTICS
84	COLLEGE PLANNING
78	TRANSFER STUDENTS
76	EDUCATIONAL FINANCE
72	STATE PROGRAMS
69	COMMUNITY COLLEGES
68	DOCTORAL THESES
65	COLLEGE FACULTY
63	CURRICULUM DEVELOPMENT
55	TEACHER EDUCATION
52	ACADEMIC ACHIEVEMENT
52	MASTER PLANS
51	GOVERNANCE
49	SUBPROFESSIONALS
47	EDUCATIONAL FACILITIES
46	COLLEGE ROLE

Figure 19
Frequency ordered descriptor
list: ERIC-RIE junior college
subset

(obtained from a printed copy), and the total number of records in the file, one could see in a few seconds a reasonably accurate estimate of the number of hits that the request should elicit. Again, this procedure would be especially valuable in "presearching" very large files.

4. NOT-*logic*. Because it usually takes precedence in the hierarchy of machine operations, *NOT*-logic may best be dealt with by assigning it a parameter of its own. If a *NOT*-term is interspersed with other terms in a parameter, the *NOT*-term may override other logical combinations in that group. The effect of this could be to negate the entire parameter, and thus turn the search into something quite different from what was intended.

Note that, in general, there is very little reason to employ *NOT*-logic until at least one search has been done, the results analyzed, and the patron's comments considered. *NOT*-logic is not designed to help one retrieve relevant items by the large-scale exclusion of other descriptors; if the search calls for "GREAT BRITAIN," but not "ENGLAND" or "SCOTLAND" or "WALES" or "NORTHERN IRELAND," obviously only "GREAT BRITAIN" is requested. If, however, it is found that much potential material on the subject of interest is often indexed with another descriptor which renders it irrelevant, then one should utilize the excluding power of *NOT*:

> INSTRUCTIONAL TELEVISION . . . etc.
> *AND*
> INSTRUCTIONAL INNOVATION . . . etc.
> *AND*
> PRIVATE SCHOOLS . . . etc.
> *NOT*
> SECONDARY GRADES

5. *Connotation of Terms.* Care must be taken to interpret the meaning of subject terms (particularly precoordinated terms) in the *context* of the system. Often there are guides to this; the *Thesaurus of ERIC Descriptors* is one which provides multiple approaches:

    a. List of descriptors groupings (52 classes) with annotations for each
    b. List of all terms contained within any specific grouping
    c. Scope notes for certain terms in the main body of the *Thesaurus*
    d. Descriptors whose connotation is actually a part of the term, as, for example, "ADJUSTMENT (TO ENVIRONMENT)" and "ARTICULATION (PROGRAM)."

Most reference librarians are familiar with this problem from their experience with assisting users at the public catalog. However, since a subject thesaurus is by definition a specialized, controlled vocabulary, the question of connotative meaning assumes somewhat more importance than it has with a "universal" subject list, such as that of the Library of Congress. "PLAY THERAPY" is given a grouping in the ERIC Thesaurus (420) which implies strongly that the connotation is "play as a psychotherapeutic aid in working with emotionally disturbed children," and several documents indexed with the term do cover this topic. However, the same term has been employed with "DRAMATIC PLAY" and "CHILDRENS GAMES," to connote "play as a vehicle for normal learning" in the Froebelian sense, a markedly different connotation.

It is when one goes outside the system imposed by one thesaurus, however, and begins to contemplate running the same request against multiple files, that the difficulties really commence. "EVALUATION" is a technical term in the ERIC system, a general term almost everywhere else. "PITCH" can refer to motion of bodies, angle of incline, quality of sound, and surfacing of roads. Other examples will readily come to mind, and they should serve to emphasize the necessity of continuous alertness on the part of the information specialist.

Summary

The cornerstone of good search formulation is the rigorous analysis of the request in terms of its main subject concepts. This should be done on paper before any Boolean logic is applied. Term frequency statistics should be consulted where available. The profile should then be formulated, with the main concepts usually linked by *AND*-logic and the terms selected to describe each main concept usually linked by *OR*-logic. Other criteria, such as exclusion of specific authors, or chronological constraints, may then be added, and the search should in general not ask for the co-occurrence of more than four factors.

8
Refinement and Reiteration

When the formulated request mirrors the statement of interest to the search analyst's satisfaction, the work of coding begins. Since this is merely the way of representing in a certain notation the logical formulation already arrived at, it is a fairly routine procedure; and since every system has its own notational and syntactical conventions, no extensive description of this phase of the operation is necessary. "Coding" in this context does not mean reducing the logical expression to an abstruse machine language or a string of binary digits; as noted in chapter 5, the computer routinely performs both of these operations. Rather, it means writing out the logically formulated profile in the search language employed by the system; the results will be a type of shorthand English, as illustrated in Appendix C. The terms are still recognizable, but the required symbols and identifications have been added.

While it is true that the prior intellectual tasks, namely subject analysis and the selection of appropriate search logic, are the more critical ones for the librarian, the coding of a search is done most efficiently by the person who formulated it. The theoretical distinction between the operations of formulating and coding is emphasized here for illustrative purposes; in

120

practice, the two are generally merged into one single exercise of profile construction, and it will always be true to some extent that *how* one may code can exert a subtle influence on *what* is being coded.

Great variation is already apparent between different systems in the degree of flexibility permitted in the coding process. Most search systems require the coding to be done on a special form, sometimes called a coding sheet. Certain identifying information will be required at the head of each profile, and this probably will have a fixed format (perhaps the equivalent of one punched card, arranged in a fixed, standard way).

Two limitations governing the way the machine-readable request is to be formatted should be expected. First, the conventions of the file to be searched must be studied. There is obviously no point in asking for "POLY-VINYL-CHLORIDE" *OR* "PVC" when the indexing rules state that no hyphens and no abbreviations are used with compound terms. Second, there will be certain constraints in the search program itself, mainly for reasons of machine efficiency and general operating economy. To prevent inordinate search costs, there may be a limit to the size of each profile. If so, that limit will be sufficiently high—say, 199 cards—that anything exceeding it could almost certainly have been expressed more succinctly by using "tighter" coding. Subject terms may have to be delimited, perhaps by quotes, in order to allow an unambiguous recognition to be made by the machine. This would be necessary, for instance, with a term such as "ARTICULATION (PROGRAM)," where the term's parentheses might otherwise be indistinguishable from logical parentheses. Each term may have to begin on a new line; ampersands may or may not be legitimate; an "end of profile" symbol may be required, and the like. These are purely syntactical conventions and should not, within very broad limits, prevent anyone from constructing an accurate, logical equivalent of the information need expressed by the patron.

When all the components of the statement of interest have been identified, rendered into a logical formulation, properly coded, and transcribed into machine-readable form (or "keyboarded"), the search is submitted to be run. What follows is outside the librarian's province, and therefore no discussion of it is presented in this book.

After a search is made, interest naturally centers upon the output. It should be anticipated that whatever the result, some further analysis will be necessary the first time, and quite possibly several times more, until the profile is "tuned" and the patron confirms that the results are right on target. To begin with the most basic contingencies, there will either be *some* output (hits) or *no* output. If the search resulted in the latter, (omitting, as implied above, any discussion of machine failure or errors in the job control instructions for the search, and assuming that the search was successfully submitted to, and processed by, the computer), and if the cause is not immediately obvious, a systematic check should be performed in ascending order as follows:

1. *Error in Translation.* This indicates something technically wrong with the way in which the question was asked, sometimes referred to as "error in syntax." The objective is to pinpoint where the search formulation failed to observe the logical conventions and syntax of the particular searching system being used. For example, if parentheses were employed, did the number of left parentheses equal the number of right? Were they correctly placed in relation to the terms and the logical operators? If any other delimiters, such as quotes, were necessary, were they all present and correct? Was the logic unambiguous? Were there any other stray typographical errors made in the syntax, such as A & & B? If the logical expressions were supposed to have brief identifying tags, or if data field numbers on the file were used in the search, were they all correct?

Errors in syntax are relatively frequent and can prove very costly if not detected. Increasingly, therefore, a search system will have a program at the beginning, known as a *diagnostic routine,* which checks for logical and syntactical errors. Even so, if one has to submit the profile, perhaps as part of a batch search, and wait until the entire run is completed before being informed that Question # 2 was rejected because it contained Standard Error # 17, "Missing Parenthesis," this is still rather tedious. The person writing the searches might, in such circumstances, suggest to the programmer that a separate machine-readable copy of the diagnostic routine be made; all new profiles could then be checked beforehand at a cost of only a few pennies per profile. If the check must be performed again as part of the actual search, little has been lost.

2. *Other typographical errors.* This encompasses not only obvious spelling errors but also incorrect use of the blank space, which is a character like any other on the keyboard. In general, there are no fully operational systems as yet which can deduce that by "EDUCATON," the writer had intended "EDUCATION." This would require the full thesaurus in machine-readable form; several are available in this fashion, including that of the ERIC system, but they are customarily used for display purposes rather than analytic ones. At present, having each subject term checked against the thesaurus would be a lengthy and expensive task, though eventually it will probably be the routine thing to do.

Similarly, if a multiword descriptor has inadvertently had an extra blank (b) inserted, as in "JUNIORbCOLLEGEbbLIBRARIES," then the computer, being totally literal, is searching for a descriptor which is so different that it might have been written backwards. This can happen very easily, as for example when one is keyboarding on a video terminal. However, it is possible to overcome this by extra programming which would instruct the computer not only to find a descriptor containing certain letters, but also to ignore blanks and other punctuation. Naturally this is more costly; moreover, it could lead to further problems (author is "JAMES, ANTHONY" or "PETLEY-JONES, DAVID") in that it would be necessary to program rules not only for the desired cases, but also for the exceptions.

3. *Search logic too restrictive.* The use of *AND*-logic should be checked, with a view to answering the question, "Can I reasonably have expected this request to produce any hits in a file of this size?" Any *NOT*-logic should also be reevaluated.

4. *Choice of descriptors.* The same question should be posited in relation to the descriptors used, at least until a solid fund of experience with the thesaurus and the system as a whole has been built up. Were the descriptors too specific or narrow? Were they correctly grouped, with synonyms in the same parameter? The thesaurus should be consulted again for alternative approaches to the topic, and the descriptor frequency list checked where possible. It should be remembered that most frequency lists refer to the master file. If an ERIC descriptor has a listed frequency in *Research in Education* of twenty, this means, at present, twenty occurrences in approximately 70,000 references, or one in 3,500. Great care obviously is needed in including this term in a current awareness search of the most recent RIE tape, which will contain about 3,500 entries.

5. *Subject coverage.* Even if the search formulation was entirely logical and correct, and the descriptors were the right ones, it is always possible that there was just no material in the file on the topic requested. The general subject scope and contents of the file should be examined again.

If, on the other hand, output *was* obtained, it should be analyzed, preferably by the librarian who formulated the profile, and later in conjunction with the patron and his original statement of interest. It is crucial to keep in mind that the question to be posed is not, "Did we get what we asked for?" (when using the computer the answer is likely to be an overwhelming, "Yes, you got exactly what you asked for") but, "Should we have asked for what we got?" In other words, is the retrieved material relevant?

The question of how relevance can be measured is one of the central issues of automated information storage and retrieval. Since the ASLIB-Cranfield experiments,[1] one of the landmarks of information science, the term "relevance" has been generally used to mean the larger judgment about a retrieved item's actual suitability in terms of the request. In an effort to assess the technical efficiency of a machine search, the twin concepts of *recall* and *precision* have been evolved. For a lucid and detailed treatment of this topic, consult F. Wilfrid Lancaster, *Information Retrieval Systems*.[2]

In a typical computer search, characterized by some complexity in the request, the resulting citations will obviously show variation in their degree of relevance. In a simple straightforward search, such as a request for all citations indexed with the term "EVENING CLASSES" there is no such problem, for everything retrieved completely fulfills the search criterion. Conversely, there can be no records in the file which match the search term and are not retrieved. At the reference desk too, a simple, uncomplicated question, "In what year did George Washington die?" can be answered with one hundred percent assurance of success; whereas for an open-ended question, such as "What material do you have on the economics of environmental protection?" the librarian has to produce a whole spectrum of different solutions and watch the patron's response to see which is most appropriate. Similarly, in a complex computerized search, the precision with which the hits fulfill the request will vary; also there is likely to be additional material in the file which the patron would have found valuable, had the question been so structured as to recall it. The latter consideration can only be truly measured by a manual search and evaluation of all the entries in the file. Thus it becomes difficult and costly to perform evaluations with files of more than about one thousand documents, and one has no choice but to use sampling. As an example of how recall and precision are calculated, let us postulate that a search has the following results:

Size of file (number of references)	100,000
Number of references relevant to the given request in file	100
Number of references actually retrieved	80
Number of retrieved references judged relevant	60

Recall is then calculated by dividing as follows:

$$\frac{\text{Number of relevant references retrieved}}{\text{Number of relevant references in file}} \quad \frac{60}{100} \ or \ 60\%$$

Precision is found by:

$$\frac{\text{Number of relevant references retrieved}}{\text{Number of references retrieved}} \quad \frac{60}{80} \ or \ 75\%.$$

Here may be clearly seen what is perhaps the single most important point about recall and precision: they are not expressed as absolutes, but as ratios. In the hypothetical example, seeing a figure which states that the search only recalled 60 percent of what it "should" have recalled, the search analyst might naturally attempt to elicit the remaining 40 percent. The ASLIB-Cranfield experiments established that in order to capture those remaining relevant references in the file, that is, to boost the recall ratio to 100 percent, it would be necessary to cast the net so wide that the precision ratio would fall sharply, causing the example to read approximately as follows (again the figures are illustrative only):

Number of relevant references in file	100
Number of references actually retrieved	500
Number of retrieved references judged relevant	100

While the recall ratio has risen to 100 percent, the precision ratio is now only 20 percent. The clear implication here is that one can, theoretically, obtain every relevant item in a file, but the effort necessary to do so (and then to sift out the relevant hits from the irrelevant) makes it virtually impossible under normal operating conditions. Conversely, any attempt to push the precision ratio up to 100 percent inevitably sends the recall ratio down: they vary inversely. This is all a matter of how broadly or narrowly the request is specified—of how many terms are employed, and how they are linked together with exclusive *AND* or inclusive *OR*. The fact that recall and precision vary inversely in most normal retrieval systems means that one can, within reasonable limits, predict how much one ratio will go down if the other is raised to a given point. An acceptable, workable balance between the two is the most that is operationally feasible. Experience suggests that any system which achieves a stable balance of about 65 percent recall with 65 percent precision is probably operating near to its best overall efficiency.[3] In any event, the librarian should carefully explain to the patron that one does not go to the computer, press a button, and watch it retrieve 100 percent of what is revelant, no more and no less. The whole process is an interplay of ratios, one against the other, with an approximation of total recall or total precision. Again it is emphasized that the concepts of recall and precision deal only with relevance in the narrow technical sense of whether or not the computer search system is performing adequately. They deliberately avoid the much hazier question of whether or not the user actually found the document or reference relevant to his needs. There is, in fact, a continuing debate about the measurement of the latter aspect of relevance.[4]

The librarian who is analyzing a completed search must be alert to these factors when assessing the output and deciding under what circumstances to refine the search formulation and run it again. Was the first version too specific, relying heavily on *AND*- or *NOT*-logic, and making very limited use of synonyms, *OR*-logic, term truncation, and other devices designed to increase one's options? This will be reflected in output consisting of a few citations which should be highly relevant to the user. Was it, by contrast, too general, with too much logical and syntactical looseness, or too many overlapping terms, especially high frequency terms joined by *OR*-logic? This will produce a great mass of hits with relatively low precision. Some will undoubtedly be acceptable, but others would cause the patron, were he simply to be given the output, to wonder what on earth the computer (and the search analyst) was doing. In either case, it should be clear why it is advantageous to know the descriptor frequencies, if at all possible. In the former instance, the patron loses the opportunity to make unexpectedly valuable "finds," to browse among material which is partially related to his main topic. In the latter, he is being asked to accept, and possibly to pay for, a heavy proportion of marginal material in order to cover the central core of the topic.

Assuming that the cause of an unsatisfactory performance in either direction is not due to some obvious error, such as writing *OR* when circumstances called for *AND,* or asking for everything in the English language, it is reasonable to say that the inverse relationship between recall and precision is not as inhibiting as it may sound. As in a traditional reference situation, users frequently do not know precisely what they want until they have had a look at material which the librarian has suggested. At the University of California at Los Angeles, the authors have processed search requests of the broadest type for librarians involved in collection development, as well as a single search request so specific that it continually produces no output. However, in the latter instance, the patron has affirmed that the search is correct and that the results are not unexpected. He is aware that very little is being written in this particular subject area, and the fact that this is confirmed by the output from a major bibliographic source is valuable information for him. Constructing computer searches is, in fact, an art, a practical art not unlike other aspects of librarianship. It is simply the modernizing of a librarian's professional skills in the handling of information.

Whether, in view of the pros and cons on both sides, a search should be generally slanted toward precision or recall, is a decision that can only be made in-house, since it involves the type of information need being served, the timing, the financial considerations, and the like. Furnishing a patron with large quantities of wide-ranging output may nullify the expectations that the popular image of the computer have engendered— the image of almost effortless speed and accuracy in retrieving what was "asked for." The user does, indeed, receive all that was asked for, but not always all that was wanted. Limiting the scope of the search will

```
QUERY ID: WATSON      NAME: MATHIES CIJE370R3      HITS    1   PAGE    1
EJ020488                                                          TE900101
PINCAS, ANITA
WRITING IN PARAGRAPHS
J IND ARTS EDUC SPECIAL ISSUE; 29; 4; 182-185.
PUB DATE: 70.
DESCRIPTORS: *ENGLISH (SECOND LANGUAGE);*PARAGRAPH
COMPOSITION;*WRITING SKILLSUSTRIAL ARTS OFFERS OPPORTUNITIES TO STUDY
NUDENT ROLE;TEACHER ROLE;CLASSROOM ENVIRONMENT;TEACHER
BACKGROUND;TEACHER EDUCATION;INSERVICE TEACHER EDUCATION  ENGL LANG
TEACHING. 24; 2; 173-178-172ENTENCE OR MAIN CLAUSE IN WHICH IT OCCURS
OR BY ANAPHORIC REFERENCE. *THE AUTHOR IDENTIFIES THREE
GROUPS;CONNECTED DISCOURSE;CURRICULUM DEVELOPMENT;EDUCATIONAL CHANGE.
THE PATTERNS OF DIFFERENT TYPES OF PARAGRAPHS ARE EXAMINED AND
SUGGESTIONS ON EFFECTIVE METHODS OF TEACHING PARAGRAPH WRITING ARE
GIVEN. (FWB)
CPU TIME:    .014 SECS.    ELAPSED TIME:    .192 SECS.
```

Figure 20
Example of a defective citation

provide fewer, more highly relevant citations, but it also will remove the opportunity to scan the sides of a topic as well as its central theme. It is on these peripheries that the serendipitous "find" occurs. And, far from computers "taking over," human judgment, in general, and professional library skills, in particular, will be more important than ever in interpreting these complex requests in a manner that will elicit the optimum mixture of recall and precision from the computer.

Finally, in evaluating output, librarians should be aware that even if all appears to go smoothly, the output might still, on rare occasions, look like the sample in figure 20. If this happens, the librarian should be prepared to point out that the library is no more responsible for the authenticity or quality of the information on computer tapes than it is for that in books. As with defective books, there may come a point when a direct complaint to the manufacturer becomes necessary. However, unlike printed media, an additional choice is open with the computer (if copyright arrangements permit); that is to have the record corrected in-house. In figure 20, for example, it would be necessary to have access to the printed issue of *Current Index to Journals in Education,* as well as to the requisite programming ability. The distributor or manufacturer may have a policy of issuing corrected versions of faulty records in update tapes. The MARC system, for example, uses a convenient code to "flag" corrected records; replacement of the defective ones can then be done automatically. However, such procedures can become expensive. The U.S. Bureau of the Census subsequently discovered errors, such as the overcounting of the nation's centenarians by about 100,000, in the 1970 census for which there are no funds to permit it to go back and retabulate. Again, the librarians' expertise in dealing with information problems as an integrated whole stands them in good stead. They have the ability to use other sources for reference and cross-checking, and thus, through accurate documentation of an error, can help to negate its ill effects.

Summary

After a search has been coded and run, the results should be scrutinized carefully. There are a number of checks which can be performed, ranging from the smallest syntactical nicety to the broadest question of relevance. Ratios of the *recall* and the *precision* of a search can be calculated, and a balance established between the *inclusive* and *exclusive* tendencies of the two.

Notes

1. Cyril W. Cleverdon, *Factors Determining the Performance of Indexing Systems,* 2 v. (Cranfield, England: College of Aeronautics, 1966).

2. F. Wilfrid Lancaster, *Information Retrieval Systems: Characteristics, Testing, and Evaluation* (New York: Wiley, 1968), chaps. 6 and 7.
3. Ibid., p. 77 (figure 22).
4. *See,* for example, D. J. Foskett, "A Note on the Concept of 'Relevance,'" *Information Storage and Retrieval* 8:77 (Apr. 1972).

part three

Other Machine-Readable Data Bases

9

MARC

Introduction

The MARC (*MA*chine *R*eadable *C*ataloging) project at the Library of Congress (LC) grew out of the recommendation made by the King Report, *Automation in the Library of Congress* (1963),[1] that methods of automating the entire flow of internal processing at the library be investigated. From the report, it was clear that a machine-readable catalog record would not only constitute a major component in this proposed development of automated processing techniques for LC, but would also be of immeasurable value to other libraries which look to the Library of Congress for national leadership, particularly in cataloging.

The subsequent years have seen two distinct phases. After the decision to accept the King Report's recommendation and to give priority to machine-readable cataloging, an .extensive pilot project involving sixteen other libraries was carefully planned, executed, and reported. The outcome of the pilot project was the MARC tape distribution service, which has already come to occupy a central place in modern library history. The second phase has been the process of learning to use MARC. This ability did not come immediately, not even to most of the libraries which had

133

participated in the pilot project. Most institutions planning to exploit MARC had considerable technical and financial preparation to do before any benefits could be realized; the format was new and reflected the experience gained in the pilot project; the data base itself was small; and considerable systems analysis was needed to assess MARC's impact on a library's existing operations. Now, one decade after the King Report, many libraries are using MARC for technical processing tasks, either directly or indirectly through the services of a bookdealer or a cooperative agency, such as the highly successful Ohio College Library Center. Simultaneously, the scope of the data base has been extended, and MARC formats have been designed for other media such as serials, films, and maps. The great work of retroactively converting LC catalog records has begun, a second major step toward fulfillment of the King Report's glittering vision of a future in which the entire LC catalog would be stored on-line and queried interactively through video terminals. (A trillion-bit storage device, which the Committee considered to be essential for such work, but which in 1963 was nonexistent, has now been built.) Most library schools are now giving the librarians of tomorrow some form of exposure to MARC; in several, it is a basic part of the teaching and research programs, often centered in specially equipped teaching laboratories or other facilities.

From these hopeful developments, it is possible to predict that another decade will see large-scale reliance on MARC in libraries. The data base itself will be a priceless resource, probably containing in excess of a million citations, and, equally important, the bibliographic format designed by the MARC team will be routinely employed in the creation of many other data bases. In fact, MARC has already been adopted as an American national standard, and, as the full extent of its capability is realized, more and more data base suppliers will not find it profitable to ignore it. We also expect that the next few years will see a quickening in the adoption of MARC as a tool for information retrieval services to library patrons. The close correspondence between a MARC record and any library's catalog record (they may differ in choice of subject headings, call number, and the like, but little variation is likely in author and title) will make possible a higher level of integrated information service than has previously been provided. The patron will receive automatic notification of new materials of interest to him in a form suitable for his personal bibliographic file, the library will have completed technical processing of the work very soon after receipt, and the patron will be able to come in and get the work with a minimum of delay, or perhaps even telephone to request that the book be checked out and sent to him. If the patron wants an older work not held in the library, national computerized networks of interlibrary loan data, also making use of MARC, will expedite an interlibrary loan.

These are only some of the more obvious potential applications of

MARC data. There are undoubtedly many others which readers can relate to their own operating situations, but enough has been said to indicate how crucial it will be to have skilled reference librarians capable of working with MARC data on a day-to-day basis.

Background

The MARC project is a recent development, which is known at least in general terms to most librarians. The following background, therefore, takes the form of a brief chronology for reference purposes. The indispensable document for historical details is *The MARC Pilot Project.*[2] It is also worth noting that throughout the developmental phase of MARC, the Council on Library Resources, which had commissioned the King Report, took a central position, funding special studies, sponsoring workshops and conferences, and assisting with the publication and dissemination of the results.

1963	The King Report recommended as a national desideratum the automation of the functions of the Library of Congress.
1964	Preliminary study of possible methods of converting the information on LC catalog cards to a machine-readable form.
1965 (Jan.)	First Conference on Machine-Readable Catalog Copy was convened at LC to consider the results of the preliminary study. Two main conclusions: a. machine-readable catalog data from LC was essential to library automation efforts, and b. a standard format was needed to allow other libraries to catalog their *own* works in a compatible mode.
1965 (Nov.)	Second Conference on Machine-Readable Catalog Copy discussed the fields to be represented in a machine-readable catalog record and a possible magnetic tape format.
1966 (Feb.)	Third Conference on Machine-Readable Catalog Copy began active planning for a pilot project. Initial coverage was to be *current English-language monographs, U.S. imprints;* sixteen libraries were selected to participate, based on type of library, geographic location, and ability to process the tapes and evaluate the results.
1966 (Oct.)	Beginning of the MARC Pilot Project, to last through June 1967.
1967 (Mar.)	MARC staff initiated review of the MARC I format and began design of MARC II.

1967 (June)   At the American Library Association annual conference, a preliminary MARC II format was presented. LC announced that the Pilot Project would be extended through June 1968, and that a full-scale, operational MARC Distribution Service would follow.

1969 (Apr.)   Announcement of a MARC format for serials (preliminary edition).

1969 (June)   MARC Distribution Service began. Coverage was extended to *all current English-language monographs* received by LC.

1970   Project RECON (REtrospective CONversion of LC catalog records to MARC format) was begun.

1972   MARC format for films was announced, and a tape distribution service was begun.

1973 (July)   First MARC serial tape available. Coverage of *current French-language* monographs was begun.

File Structure and Characteristics

The complete, official documentation has been published by the Information Science and Automation Division of ALA.[3]

The file structure was designed to represent an LC catalog card, with its extremely intricate bibliographic structure. In most respects this is far more complicated than the bibliographic citation customarily found in an abstracting and indexing serial, as seen in the ERIC files. Figure 21 shows the fields currently defined, together with their identifiers, called "tags."

Tagging is the central concept in files where it is desirable to allow each field to have only the amount of space it needs, rather than to make it occupy a predetermined, fixed length. As the name suggests, a "tag" is merely an identification label to signal to the computer what is coming next. For efficiency of processing, a *directory* of all the tags contained in any one record, showing the length of each field, is assembled and placed at the beginning of the tape record, as a kind of "table of contents." The technical conventions governing the ways in which records are stored together on a tape are not of concern here. Even a cursory look will indicate how many possible combinations of conditions can occur in representing a catalog card, and therefore how many decisions a MARC editor must make and record. Of the seventy or so defined data fields, fifty are currently in use. Twenty-nine of these may contain their data in one of several forms. In addition, thirty-one of the fields may consist of subfields, of which as many as eleven have been specified for certain fields, and, in many cases, a field or subfield may be repeated as often as necessary. Each of these myriad contingencies must be uniquely coded in order to generate a correctly formatted MARC II monographic catalog record.

Control Numbers

*0 1 0   LC Card Number
*0 1 1   Linking LC Card Number
 0 1 5   National Bibliography Number
*0 1 6   Linking NBN
*0 1 7   U.S. Copyright Number
 0 2 0   Standard Book Number
*0 2 1   Linking SBN
 0 2 5   Overseas Acquisitions Number
*0 2 6   Linking OAN Number
*0 3 5   Local System Number
*0 3 6   Linking Local Number
 0 4 0   Cataloging Source
 0 4 1   Languages
*0 4 2   Search Code
*0 4 3   Geographic Area Code

Knowledge Numbers

 0 5 0   LC Call Number
 0 5 1   Copy Statement
 0 6 0   NLM Call Number
 0 7 0   NAL Call Number
*0 7 1   NAL Copy Statement
*0 7 2   NAL Subject Category Number
*0 8 0   UDC Number
*0 8 1   BNB Classification Number
 0 8 2   Dewey Decimal Classification No.
*0 8 6   Supt. of Documents Classification
*0 9 0   Local Call Number

Main Entry

1 0 0   Personal Name
1 1 0   Corporate Name
1 1 1   Conference or Meeting
1 3 0   Uniform Title Heading

Supplied Titles

2 4 0   Uniform Title
2 4 1   Romanized Title
*2 4 2   Translated Title

Title Paragraph

2 4 5   Title
2 5 0   Edition Statement
2 6 0   Imprint

Collation

3 0 0   Collation
3 5 0   Bibliographic Price
*3 6 0   Converted Price

*The Library of Congress will not supply
 data for these fields at present

Series Notes

4 0 0   Personal Name-Title (Traced Same)
4 1 0   Corporate Name-Title (Traced Same)
4 1 1   Conference-Title (Traced Same)
4 4 0   Title (Traced Same)
4 9 0   Series Untraced or Traced
        Differently

Bibliographic Notes

5 0 0   General Notes
5 0 1   "Bound With" Note
5 0 2   Dissertation Note
*5 0 3   Bibliographic History Note
5 0 4   Bibliography Note
5 0 5   Contents Note (Formatted)
*5 0 6   "Limited Use" Note
5 2 0   Abstract or Annotation

Subject Added Entries

6 0 0   Personal Name
6 1 0   Corporate Name (excluding
        political jurisdiction alone)
6 1 1   Conference or Meeting
6 3 0   Uniform Title Heading

LC Subject Headings

6 5 0   Topical
6 5 1   Geographic Names

Other Subject Headings

*6 6 0   NLM Subject Headings (MESH)
*6 7 0   NAL Subject Headings
*6 9 0   Local Subject Heading Systems

Other Added Entries

7 0 0   Personal Name
7 1 0   Corporate Name
7 1 1   Conference or Meeting
7 3 0   Uniform Title Heading
7 4 0   Title Traced Differently

Series Added Entries

8 0 0   Personal Name-Title
8 1 0   Corporate Name-Title
8 1 1   Conference or Meeting-Title
8 4 0   Title

Figure 21
MARC variable field tags

"Main Entry, Personal Name" is an example of a field which has been analyzed into the different possible forms in which the information can occur:

Field 100—MAIN ENTRY, PERSONAL NAME
will be one of four types:

(100)	0	Forename only
(100)	1	Single surname
(100)	2	Multiple surname
(100)	3	Name of family

The added digit is called an *Indicator*.

"Imprint" is an example of a variable field composed of subfields:

Field 260—IMPRINT

has subfields:

   a   Place of Publication
   b   Publisher
   c   Date

These represent the possible components of a field, the different types of information to be found there. As noted above, subfields may be repeated where necessary: Place of Publication given as "London and New York" would cause Field 260 to have the structure "a, a, b, c."

It is important to realize, however, that a full MARC record is not limited merely to the actual bibliographic data describing the document, complex as that may be. The variable fields are preceded by a *Leader,* giving technical data such as the record status (new, corrected, or deleted); a *Record Directory,* or table of contents, which itself must obviously be variable length; and *Control Fields,* mainly of fixed length, containing an amalgam of numerical, fixed length codes and indicators, some of which are in the record, others of which are not. For example, the LC card number, which is the sequencing number of the MARC file, is given here; so also are brief code numbers, usually "0" or "1," indicating whether the work is a biography, or a festschrift, or a work of fiction, or has an index, and so on. This is an excellent device for rapidly identifying publications by these various criteria, since it circumvents the need for a complicated computer program designed to search about in the variable fields, trying to deduce from the presence or absence of certain words whether the work has an index, or is fictional, and the like. The Leader also has some blank spaces into which any individual organization can insert codes of internal significance. For example, the University of California inserts a "campus code," showing at which campuses the work is held.

The MARC II format, being a highly sophisticated and flexible bibliographic tool, is capable of being put to an almost endless variety of uses. The fact that it has to be so complicated in order to adequately represent the possible contents of any library catalog card is an implicit tribute to the care and completeness with which librarians have been making their bibliographic records over the years.

The excellent theoretical work that went into designing the MARC II Communications Format has ensured the relative stability of the system, although numerous revisions have been necessary due to the growth of the file and of the system as a whole. This is reflected in the treatment of romanized titles, shared cataloging, dates of republication, and foreign currencies. The list of Language Codes has already increased from 171 to

262, but the Place of Publication code list has remained almost constant at 314 (USA, UK, Canada, and USSR may be subdivided). Even though coverage has until very recently been limited to English-language monographs, the MARC character set now contains more than thirty diacritics, and the imperatives of scientific publishing have prompted the inclusion of sub- and superscript notation, plus Greek α, β, and γ. An "encoding level" code has recently been added to the Leader to indicate the probable degree of completeness of the record, by flagging any entries which were *not* based on a physical inspection of the item in question.

Format Recognition

There can be little doubt that the directory-string type of record with variable-length, repeating fields is the most appropriate intellectual solution to the problems of bibliographic file formats, but the complexities which this approach entails in terms of processing, both by humans and computers, should be self-evident. Therefore, faced not only with the current records entering the MARC system, but also with the prospect of having to convert a staggering volume of retrospective records, the MARC staff pioneered the design of computerized systems to alleviate this burden. What has become known as *Automatic Field Recognition* enables the computer to generate a correctly formatted record from the basic input data; by reducing processing time for variable, repeating field records, this has obviated one of the principal reasons for working in fixed fields.

The underlying idea of the process is surprisingly simple: give the computer a way of identifying any one part of the record, and it can deduce much of the rest of the record structure by the application of logical tests. Of the few data fields which will occur in 100 percent of the cases, the beginning of the Collation field has been judged easiest to ascertain. Immediately preceding this must be the Title paragraph. The following listing[5] shows the six cases that can occur:

Case	First Field	Second Field	Third Field	Fourth Field	Fifth Field
1	TP	CP			
2	CN	TP	CP		
3	ME	TP	CP		
4	CN	ME	TP	CP	
5	ME	UT	TP	CP	
6	CN	ME	UT	TP	CP

Where: CN   Call Number
ME   Main Entry
TP   Title Paragraph
UT   Uniform Title—Type 1
CP   Collation Paragraph

The Collation search begins in the second field encountered, and the record is built up by a "look-back-then-look-forward" procedure, using such tests as searching for a match from among a given array of keywords likely to occur in this or that field, or examining the alphanumeric structure of an element. For example, a Bibliographic Note field containing a term such as "Thesis" or "Dissertation" will automatically be tagged as Field 502, Dissertation Note. Similarly, when the computer reads "vi, 328p" it finds that this matches a certain structural pattern which it has been told occurs in Field 300, subfield a: Collation (Pagination). Naturally, as Henriette Avram says, "The efficiency of automatically determining a condition that rarely occurs. . .must be measured against the computer time expended to look for that particular condition."[6] If the machine can assign the first two digits of a three digit tag, therefore, it may be told to go on to the next field. If the computer can in this manner accomplish even 80 to 90 percent of the drudgery of formatting these complex bibliographic records, the saving in time and effort is considerable.

External Characteristics (MARC Current Monographs)

Size:	over 240,000 records by mid-1973
Growth Rate:	approximately 6,000 entries per month by mid-1973
Cost:	$1,000 per year
Frequency of Issue:	a subscription may be for weekly, quarterly, semiannual or annual tapes
Documentation:	*MARC Manuals Used by the Library of Congress,* 2d ed. Prepared by the Information Systems Office, Library of Congress. Chicago: American Library Assn., Information Science and Automation Division, 1970. $12.50 (This has since been supplemented by looseleaf sheets sent automatically to tape subscribers.)
Programs:	none available from manufacturer. The MARC file is so complex that most institutions using it have written their own series of programs for processing it.

Notes

1. *Automation and the Library of Congress* (Washington: Library of Congress, 1963). ("The King Report.")
2. *The MARC Pilot Project* (Final Report), prepared by Henriette D. Avram, Project Director (Washington: Library of Congress, 1968).

3. *MARC Manuals Used by the Library of Congress,* 2d ed. (Chicago: American Library Assn., Information Science and Automation Div., 1970).

4. Ibid., "Books—A MARC Format," p. 42.

5. *Format Recognition Process for MARC Records: A Logical Design* (Chicago: American Library Assn., Information Science and Automation Div., 1970).

6. Ibid., p. 1.

10

The 1970 Census

Introduction

The United States Census of 1970 constitutes an enormous data base of numerical information, undoubtedly the most sophisticated statistical profile of a nation which has ever been generated. It is clear that 1970 was a landmark year in the development of the United States Census, marking the first overall use of "mail out, mail back" methods for the metropolitan areas, which contain 60 percent of the American population, and the first time that complete statistical summary information was available in machine-readable form as a direct by-product of the processing of the questionnaires. Although census data were put onto tape by the Bureau of the Census in 1960 to do the printing of standard tables, complete summary data were not available. Several agencies then began to keypunch the data in those tables for machine use, while at the Census Bureau, tapes containing this same information were being put into storage. It was in order to avoid a recurrence of this, while at the same time making much more data available, that the distribution of complete summary data, up to the limits of the laws of confidentiality, was planned from the start of the 1970 census operation.

All the signs indicate that this will be a "gold mine" of valuable information for many years to come, since not only will it take at least five to seven years to assimilate the 1.95 billion statistical facts in this census, but also the appearance of the 1980 census, far from rendering this one obsolete, will give it a new and vigorous lease on life, as comparative studies (longitudinal analyses) are done to see how the nation has changed in ten years. There seems little doubt that librarians and other information specialists will be meeting a broader-based demand for this data base than for any other now in view. This will take the form of more complex requests for reference information than have been typical in the past. It will involve more complicated documentation materials, such as maps, charts, file description manuals, computer program documentation, technical announcements, tabulations, and geographic cross-indexes. Furthermore, libraries may be called upon to circulate or otherwise provide copies of portions of the census and associated files on computer tape, and the reference librarian will need to know how to respond when asked to provide or arrange for computational service. Therefore it is highly desirable for reference librarians to have an understanding of the scope, contents, and organization of the machine-readable 1970 census, whether they will be directly responsible for running searches on it or not.

Background

The following is an overview of some of the principal factors which contributed to the appearance of a machine-readable census in 1970:

1. *The growing and varied use of census statistics by government, business, and academic communities.* This is so obvious that it scarcely needs comment, as many librarians in reference work can testify.

2. *The changing character of the census-taking and -publishing process.* In recent years the trend has been away from the utilization of professional census-takers and toward large-scale self-enumeration. These "mail out, mail back" methods have led to new and increasingly complex systems of geographic coding, now encompassing the city-block level, of which the average population is around ninety people. In addition to the basic housing and population questions asked of everyone (a 100 percent sample), there has been increased use of supplementary questions, which are asked of five, fifteen, or twenty percent samples, in order to gather further socioeconomic data of a more general nature. Simultaneously, there has been a progression in the methods of tabulation, from the earliest hand tallies, to automatic tabulating equipment, and to computers. It was a Census Bureau employee, Herman Hollerith, who invented the punched card, which was first used for the 1890 census; since that time the bureau

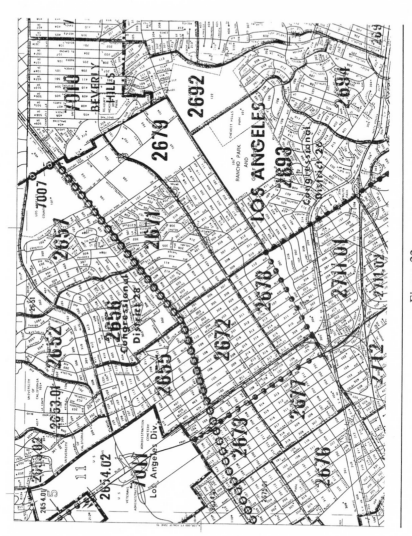

Figure 22
Portion of 1970 Census tract map

has consistently been in the forefront of research and development of automatic tabulating methods. Because larger amounts of census data are being
gathered, it follows that much more can be made publicly available; because the data are gathered and stored in a computer-processible form,
it is logical (indeed, given the sheer volume, inevitable) that it should be
made available in the same way. Hence, the 1970 census comprises not
only the conventionally published returns (the aggregational tabulations
which were all that were available in past years) but also small-area totals
and actual sample questionnaires for survey research, and the like. As has
been the case since 1790, the Census Bureau releases no data which would
identify individuals.

   3. *The Census Bureau's acceptance of its role as a service agency.* This
has not been a sudden change of policy, but rather a developing awareness
that its long-time role of data deliverer has been thrust into a new dimen-
sion with the decision to release complete summary data on computer tapes
and microfilm as well as the traditional printed tabulations. As examples,
we have:

   a. The New Haven Census Use Study, 1967–68. This was a bureau-
      sponsored research study to explore current uses and future needs in
      small-area data handling. A special local census was done and the
      project then investigated such concerns as the interrelation of census
      data with other state and local data, the level of detail and the form
      in which census data could best be made available to local users, and
      cooperative data collection between the bureau and state, local and
      other federal agencies. A sequence of reports dealt with geographic
      coding techniques for local use, data needs of local agencies, inter-
      relation of census data with local health data for health service plan-
      ning, and data uses in urban planning, school administration, and
      transportation system planning.

   b. SCRIS (Southern California Regional Information Study). A direct
      outgrowth of the New Haven study, aimed at examining the problems
      of census data use in a large metropolitan area. A major task, both
      in New Haven and Los Angeles, has been the creation of a means
      whereby census data at the smallest level (one city block, left or
      right side of the street) can be correlated with other urban files of
      data, such as sanitation, land parcel, school district, public utilities,
      traffic patterns, and crime. This is done by a technique called DIME
      —Dual Independent Map Encoding—together with an Address
      Coding Guide to the area and computer programs to match the two
      types of record.

   c. The Census Bureau's offer to produce special tabulations on demand
      and at user expense. These are defined as tabulations which require

retabulating the census basic record tapes, and therefore they are carried out only by bureau personnel. Following the substantial demand for such tabulations from the 1960 census, the bureau has established an agency known as the Central Users' Service to take over the task of providing and coordinating these activities. Costs of these tabulations from the 1960 census ranged from $500 to $100,000, with an average of $10,000. They are primarily for researchers requiring geographic or subject content precision unobtainable from the released data.

    d. The Census Bureau's development of processing programs. Five separate programs have been written by the bureau to read and display user-selected data items, accompanied by the description of that data item as printed in the technical documentation.

    e. The Census Bureau's advance workshops and seminars, and its efforts to provide liaison between proposed census tape processing centers by such means as newsletters.

In all of this, the constitutional imperatives of basic population counting for electoral reapportionment have not been forgotten by the bureau, but are now just the first in an immense range of urgent socioeconomic applications of census data.

File Structure and Characteristics

For complete, official documentation, the *1970 Census Users' Guide* should be consulted.[1]

Following are summaries of the contents of each count; figure 23 gives a tabulation of the counts, together with their tentative availability and the number of reels as first estimated by the bureau. Delays occurred, however, and the original target dates were not fully accurate.

1. *First Count Summary Tapes* were the first series of tapes available to the public. These tapes contained about 400 cells of final, complete-count population and housing data, summarized in File A for enumeration districts (in conventional enumeration areas) or blockgroups (in portions of mail census areas having Address Coding Guides), and in File B for states, counties, minor civil divisions or census county divisions, places and congressional districts. The term "place," as used in the census of population and housing, refers to "a concentration of population, regardless of the existence of legally prescribed units, powers, or functions."[2]

The population subjects tabulated include age, sex, color, marital status, and relationship to head of household. Housing subjects include tenure of occupied housing units, vacancy status, number of units in structure,

Name of file	Coverage (1)	Smallest geographic area — In file (2)	Average population size (3)	Approximate number in U.S. (4)	Approximate Number of data cells for each geographic area (5)	Tentative timing (6)	File subdivisions (7)	Approximate reels for U.S. (IBM 7-channel 556 CPI) [2] (8)
1st Count..	100%	Blockgroup/	820	235,000 ED's and Blockgroups	400	Sept.-Dec. 1970	File A: BG or ED Summaries File B: State, County, MCD(CCD), MCD-Place, Place, Congressional District	125 62
2nd Count..	100%	Tract/MCD(CCD)	Tract: 4,000 MCD's: 200- to one million+	Tracts 34,600 MCD's (CCD's) 35,000	3,500	Oct. 1970 to Apr. 1971	File A: Tract Summaries File B: State, County, MCD(CCD), Places, SMSA, and Component Areas	112 167
3rd Count..	100%	Block	90	1,500,000	250	Jan.-July 1971	Not applicable	266
4th Count..	20% 15% 5%	Tract/MCD(CCD)	Tract: 4,000 MCD's: 200- to one million+	Tracts 34,600 MCD's (CCD's) 35,000	13,000 (File A & B, and Places) 30,000 File C (except Places)	Jan.-Oct. 1971	File A: Tract Summaries File B: MCD(CCD) Summaries File C: State, County, Places, SMSA, and Component Areas	pop. -162 hous. -214 pop. -176 hous. -236 pop. -104 hous. -102
5th Count..	20% 15% 5%	3- or 5-digit ZIP area	260,000 (3-digit areas) 10,000 (5-digit areas in SMSA's)	788 (3-digit areas) 12,500[3] (5-digit areas in SMSA's)	800	July 1971	File A: 3-digit ZIP area File B: 5-digit ZIP areas in SMSA's	1 12
6th Count..	20% 15% 5%	Pop.-Cities of 100,000+ Hous.-Cities of 50,000+	500,000	132 (100,000+) 333 (50,000+)	Pop. 150,000 Hous. 110,000	Mar.-Oct. 1971	Pop.-Metr.Counties, Non-Metr. Counties 50,000+, Cities 100,000+, Central Cities, SMSA's. Hous.-State, Metr. Counties Non-Metr. Counties 50,000+, Cities 50,000+, Central Cities, SMSA's.	pop. -184 hous. -131

[1] Additional summary tape files will be developed subsequently.
[2] Summary tape files will also be available in 7- or 9-channel 800 CPI.
[3] Data will be tabulated for the population in 5-digit areas that fall within SMSA's. There is a total of 39,000 5-digit areas in the U.S.

Figure 23

Public use summary computer tape files
of the 1970 Population and Housing Census

rooms, plumbing facilities, basement, telephone, value, and contract rent. Many tabulations are cross-classified by the categories "Total," "White," and "Negro." First count File A is contained on about 106 reels of tape for the nation and File B on about fifty-seven reels, all files being issued by state.

2. *Second Count Summary Tapes* also have two file subdivisions: File A, containing about 3,500 cells of complete-count population and housing data summarized for each census tract, and File B, containing the same 3,500 data cells summarized for states, counties, minor civil divisions or census county divisions, places, and Standard Metropolitan Statistical Areas (SMSAs). Data for urban and rural parts of states, counties, and SMSAs are also available in File B. The Second Count tapes contain the same subjects as the First Count tapes but in much greater detail, due to the decrease in geographic size from census tract to block group. Second Count File A consists of 103 reels of tape for the nation and File B about 152 reels. Again, all files are issued by state.

3. *Third Count Summary Tapes* contain 250 cells of complete-count population and housing data for each city block in urbanized areas and other areas which have contracted for block statistics, issued on 238 reels for the nation. Note that these tapes contain fewer data items than are carried on the tapes for larger areas, but considerably more, particularly population characteristics, than were available in 1960 or were printed in 1970.

4. *Fourth Count Summary Tapes* contain twenty, fifteen, and five percent sample population and housing characteristics such as education, occupation, income, citizenship, vocational training, and household equipment and facilities. This count is organized into the following three file subdivisions: File A contains sample data for census tracts (sample data summaries are not available for areas smaller than census tracts); File B contains minor civil division or census county division sample summaries; and File C includes summaries for state, counties, SMSAs, and places. Both Files A and B and places in File C have 13,00 data cells summarized for each census geographic area. File C, excluding places, contains some 30,000 data cells for each area. Fourth Count tapes, also issued by state, are contained on 859 reels of tape for the entire nation.

5. *Fifth Count Summary Tapes* contain population and housing sample data summaries for ZIP Code areas; the allocation of data to these areas was accomplished (as accurately as possible) by prorating enumeration district sample counts to one or more corresponding ZIP Code areas. Approximately 800 data cells are tabulated for each ZIP Code area. Data are shown at the five-digit ZIP level for ZIP areas entirely within SMSA boundaries, and at the three-digit ZIP level for the entire United States.

One reel of tape contains summaries for all three-digit areas for the nation, and an additional twelve reels are needed for summaries for the five-digit areas. No census data summaries for individual ZIP Code areas will be printed.

6. *Sixth Count Summary Tapes* provide detailed tabulations and cross classifications of sample population and housing characteristics for states, SMSAs (metropolitan counties), nonmetropolitan counties of 50,000, and larger cities, representing considerably more data than are available in the preceding counts. The Sixth Count is divided into population and housing subfiles. For the nation, the population subfile comprises about 184 tape reels and the housing subfile 131 reels.

7. *Public Use Samples.* Virtually all the publicly available data from the census are summary data, rather than basic data about individual persons or households. Samples of basic data for large areas are, however, being made available for statistical purposes.

Public Use Samples (P.U.S.)

In 1960, the Bureau of the Census made available on tape or punched cards the separate records of the population characteristics of approximately 180,000 individuals, comprising a 0.1 percent sample of the population of the United States. The information contained on the records comprised a selection of the characteristics of persons enumerated in the twenty-five percent sample; consequently it was a 1/250 sample of the twenty-five percent.

This sample enabled users during the 1960s to prepare analytical tabulations of the characteristics of the population of the United States. The name and address information of the respondents, and certain of the more detailed items, such as place of residence, were not revealed. Data in these samples were used by a number of university, government, and private research organizations. The sample was also used as training material in social science departments of many colleges and universities.

Similar samples have been determined from the returns of the 1970 census; in fact, the total Public Use Sample program has been greatly expanded. The intent is to make the samples much more appropriate for the analysis of subgroups defined by geographic or demographic considerations. The basic elements of the Public Use Sample project are as follows:

1. There are a total of six basic P.U.S. files, each containing sample records for one percent of the population, or roughly two million individuals.
2. No names or addresses appear in the file. Geographic codes identify only areas (that is, states, SMSAs, or areas defined by a set of geographic identifiers) with more than 250,000 population.

3. All of the characteristics of people and households recorded in the census sample basic records are on the P.U.S. records. Details on place-of-residence, place-of-work, and very high income are limited to avoid identification of a particular individual.
4. Records are organized on a household-by-household basis so that characteristics of the various family members may be interrelated and associated with housing unit characteristics. Sampled vacant units and persons in group quarters are also present in the file.
5. The user may obain a P.U.S. file drawn either from the fifteen percent sample records or the five percent sample records. A one percent P.U.S. file from the fifteen percent sample records will in fact be $\frac{1}{15}$ of all such records, and likewise $\frac{1}{5}$ of the five percent sample records.
6. The user has the option of obtaining a P.U.S. file including "Neighborhood Characteristics," a set of social indicators which allow comparison of the individual's characteristics with information about the kind of neighborhood he lives in. These neighborhoods will not be identified, but will represent areas roughly the size of census tracts.

Naturally, the foregoing is only a basic sketch of what is in the file; the full description runs to about 350 pages. Note that the census has a series of *suppression indicators,* to show, for example, whether an item is never suppressed, whether individual elements in a table have been suppressed, or whether a whole tabulation has been suppressed. To summarize the levels at which data will be available:

City blocks (left or right side of street)
Block groups *or* Enumeration districts
Census tracts
SMSAs (Standard Metropolitan Statistical Areas) *or* Counties, Municipalities, Minor Civil Divisions or Places
ZIP Code areas
State
Nation

External Characteristics (Summary Tapes)

Size: Six counts, as above. Approximately thirty times as much data as will appear in printed form, on some 2,054 reels of tape from the bureau (it is possible to get this down to under 200 reels simply by compressing the data—eliminating blanks, removing record-padding with zero, and so forth).

Cost: Census Bureau processing charge, $70 per reel (includes the cost of the physical reel).

Documentation: *1970 Census Users' Guide*—Parts I and II. U.S. Department of Commerce, Bureau of the Census, 1970. $4.

Several series of Bureau publications. These include:
Small Area Data Notes
Data Access Descriptions
Census Use Studies (New Haven and Southern California studies).

Programs: The Census Bureau's Data Access and Use Laboratory has developed a set of programs (DAULIST) for processing the First through Fifth Counts. Available through the Central Users' Service of the bureau, these programs print user-selected data items with the appropriate English language descriptions for selected geographic areas. Data may also be aggregated into larger areas.

The cost is $70 per program (DAULIST comprises five programs in total) which includes the physical reel and the documentation. Programs are written in FORTRAN and COBOL and require an IBM 360 computer running under DOS, the Disk Operating System.

Several of the general program packages for processing statistical data also can be used—IBM's SPSS (Statistical Package for the Social Sciences), UCLA's BMD (Biomedical) package, and the like. In addition, many software companies, universities, and other agencies are producing basic and specialized programs tailored to the census.

Notes

1. *1970 Census Users' Guide*, pts. 1 and 2 (Washington: U.S. Dept. of Commerce, Bureau of the Census, 1970).
2. *1970 Census Users' Guide*, pt. 1, p. 80.

11

Other
Bibliographic
Files:
A Cross-Section

Introduction

By June 1971, at the time of the ALA Preconference Institute at Dallas, Texas, of which this book is an outcome, there were already in existence enough computer-readable bibliographic data bases to enable any reference librarian in science and technology to deploy all or several of them, at need, as an integrated part of a library's bibliographic service. In fact, one of the problems facing the Preconference planning committee and the authors was how far to go, or not to go, in surveying the broad range of available data bases for an event lasting only a day and a half and at the inevitable cost of providing only minimal information about each. As a compromise, those files and services that could not be included were brought to the notice of participants by the distribution, on ERIC microfiches, of a *Survey of Scientific-Technical Tape Services,* compiled by Kenneth Carroll and published jointly by the American Society for Information Science and the American Institute of Physics in 1970. (*See* the section of this chapter entitled Bibliography of Data Base Listings.) This served the double purpose of providing a bibliographical description of some fifty files, and of showing the participants a typical product of the system that had been chosen as the working example for the Preconference program.

Since that time, the trend not only toward the computerized production of printed abstracting and indexing serials, but also toward the increasing availability of the resultant machine-readable data bases as marketable products in their own right, has accelerated and shows every sign of continuing to do so for the foreseeable future. A recent update of Carroll's survey, edited by Schneider, Gechman, and Furth for ASIS, has the title *Survey of Commercially Available Computer-Readable Bibliographic Data Bases*. It lists eighty-one available resources (with an appreciably higher proportion of them originating from Europe than earlier surveys have shown) and is, at this time, the best single source of standard data about the content and publication of these files. Any librarian who actively contemplates initiating a computer-based reference service, whether by acquisition of tapes or not, and indeed anyone desiring a perspective on this whole rapidly evolving area, will find this document well worth consulting.

We mention these surveys to draw attention to the fact that magnetic tapes are beginning to develop their own bibliographic support structure. Naturally, it will be many years before the multiple bibliographic access now possible for the person desiring information on a current book is also obtainable with respect to a tape file, but we are of the belief that it is emphatically wrong to wait until hundreds and even thousands of such files exist before beginning to exert bibliographic control over them. With this in mind, we have made a start on two other bibliographic desiderata for these expensive, complex, but increasingly indispensable sources of current information—namely a critical bibliography in narrative form, and a bibliography of bibliographies. Both are merely prototypes of what we believe to be necessary and useful parts of any full spectrum of bibliographic control. At the least they can serve as a basis for more complete compilations in the future. Readers and reviewers should feel free to criticize them so that we may find out more accurately what is really needed; any suggestions or additions or comments about the need for quite different types of bibliographic information will be welcome. There is opportunity here for true professional dialogue, the outcome of which will benefit librarians and other information specialists everywhere. If interest appears to warrant it, such feedback could be submitted to a publication such as *RQ* for dissemination to the profession as a whole.

The critical bibliography, which aims to avoid reiterating most of the information in the ASIS survey, deals with ten data bases from the mainstream of what is now available. The chief reason more were not included is the simple pragmatic one that gathering together the necessary information for more was impossible in the time at our disposal. Neither of the authors nor, we suspect, anyone else has yet had the opportunity for first-hand acquaintance with all the files in, for example, the recent ASIS survey.

At the present time no one person can make a comprehensive evaluation of the whole range of machine-readable bibliographic resources in the way that traditional bibliographic surveys of printed sources have been made. Nevertheless, there is a need for such information, which must come from those librarians actually working with this or that data base. It is for this reason that we repeat our invitation for any and all comments on this admittedly small-scale first attempt. One highly desirable undertaking which comes immediately to mind is the extension of evaluative summaries, such as are given here, to the many information services which do not involve acquisition of the tapes; that is, where the manufacturers or creators of the file perform or provide search services, such as the *Dissertation Abstracts* DATRIX service, or MEDLARS. Not a few of these are provided by organizations which also do release their tapes (Institute for Scientific Information, American Geological Institute, *Psychological Abstracts* Information Service, among others).

The second section of this chapter, Bibliography of Data Base Listings, itemizes in chronological order publications known to the authors which contain lists of machine-readable data bases. These are mostly, but not entirely, concerned with bibliographic files that are now generally available. Any additions to this list also are welcome.

Evaluative Comments on Ten Data Bases

BA-Previews (Biological Abstracts)

The magnetic tape version of *Biological Abstracts* began in January 1969 and is known as *BA-Previews*. Like *CA-Condensates,* discussed later in this chapter, this data base provides bibliographic citations but substitutes keywords for the abstracts. As a further tool for automated searching, the code numbers belonging to the record's entry in the "Cross Index" and "Biosystematic (i.e., taxonomic) Index" in the printed publications are also included. Thus, instead of searching alphabetically through those indexes and making manual coordinations (always a clumsy procedure), one can specify the pertinent numerical codes as part of a machine search. A *BA-Previews* subscription supplies a *BA* tape which is issued semimonthly plus a *BioResearch Index* (BRI) tape, issued monthly.

As the designations "previews" and "condensates" make clear, both the *BA* and *CA* files in machine-readable form are not being marketed strictly as replacements for the printed journals, which remain the only source for the investigator who must see the abstract. Obviously this point was not lost on the manufacturers. However, there are indications that the decision to make this differentiation between the printed and machine-readable versions may have been short-sighted. On the face of it, the "essential" information is being furnished, the purpose being more rapid access than is possible with the printed abstract journal. This generally works very well where the primary journal is readily available; but where it is not, the abstract may be the crucial link in the information chain, and the tape service then becomes a secondary source that cites primary information not yet available (i.e., the printed abstract). Furthermore, the argument of a vast gain in efficiency and economy by not supplying full abstracts on tape is becoming increasingly less valid. In the first place, the whole abstract certainly is put onto tape at the time the basic transfer of information is made from data input sheets to a machine-readable record. In such operations, the printer is now routinely handed a tape to control the computerized typesetting process. Secondly, the costs of storing an abstract on tape are coming down as, for example, greater and greater storage densities are attained. To regard computerized information as an addition to the printed source, rather than as a highly miniaturized replacement for it, is to negate one of the main long-term benefits of using tape storage for these inherently time-limited summaries of new knowledge.

Biological Abstracts is growing at approximately 240,000 records per year, or about 10,000 per semimonthly tape. The file is furnished under one of two possible arrangements, lease or license. The former allows one to use the tapes for in-house searching, while the latter permits the licensee also to act as a center serving outsiders. The base fee is currently $5,000 per year, with royalties payable to *BA* by licensed search centers at the rate of $10 per profile searched for outside users per year. The cost of the physical reels is extra in both cases. The backfiles cost $3,800 per year for 1969 to 1971, inclusive, and $5000 for 1972. To this must be added a variable usage charge according to the nature of the services provided. A sample tape is available to bona fide potential users at no charge.

CA-Condensates (Chemical Abstracts Service)

As has been previously noted, Chemical Abstracts Service is currently providing a million new *Chemical Abstracts* citations every three years or so, which means a bibliography of new literature on and relating to chemistry, averaging some six to seven thousand items per *week*. A computer-readable version of this vast outpouring of reference data has been available since mid-1968, under the name *CA-Condensates*. It is thus called because, mainly for reasons of computer processing efficiency, it provides a condensed form of the corresponding printed entry in *Chemical Abstracts;* full bibliographic data is given, but the abstract is replaced by a set of keywords drawn from it.

Chemical Abstracts Service now publishes a whole family of machine-readable data bases in a "Standard Distribution Format," which means that "whenever a data element is included in two or more of the CAS computer-readable information services, the identification and content conventions for that data element will be identical in all of the services."[1]

The *CA-Condensates* tapes are numbered according to the printed volume and issue they represent (or will represent, since, like most machine-readable bibliographies, they customarily arrive several weeks ahead of their corresponding printed issues). This follows the Chemical Abstracts convention whereby an odd-numbered issue contains material on organic chemistry and biochemistry, while an even-numbered issue the following week contains material on inorganic chemistry, physical chemistry, chemical engineering, and the like.

Tapes are furnished under one of two possible arrangements, lease or license. The former allows one to use the tapes for in-house searching, while the latter permits the licensee also to act as a center serving outsiders. This entails a lower subscription fee than the simple lease agreement, but also involves a royalty payment to CAS (presently 1¢ per "hit" delivered to the user). The CAS brochure, which appears annually, lists all the agencies, both in the United States and other countries, operating as licensed centers. A sample tape is offered as part of an "evaluation package" which costs $60. Backfiles are sold at the same annual rate as the current tapes.

Apart from the size and scope of the data base, which alone ensures this system a position of leadership in the world of scientific information, *CA-Condensates* has several other strong points: the weekly frequency of tapes, the relative stability of the system; a high level of file documentation, and a reasonable price (by present standards in this activity) of $4,400 for lease, or $1,600 plus royalties for license, as of mid-1973. The cost of the physical reels is extra in both instances. However, the provision of only a condensed version of the printed publication is a limitation which it shares with several of the largest bibliographic data bases (as, for example, the previously mentioned *BA-Previews*).

CAIN (National Agricultural Library)

The National Agricultural Library (NAL) issues *CA*taloging and *IN*dexing information in machine-readable form as the *CAIN* data base. *CAIN* provides references which appear in print in the following sources: *Bibliography of Agriculture, National Agricultural Library Catalog,* and *American Bibliography of Agricultural Economics.* Coverage goes well beyond the narrow study of agriculture (such as animal husbandry, plant science, entomology) and into its broader ramifications, among which are included economics, sociology, ecology, and engineering. Thus, while *CAIN* is characteristically the primary tool for only a relatively small user community, it can profitably be searched as a second-level resource for those requiring information on any of a wide range of subjects in the physical, biomedical, and social sciences.

The file encompasses data from approximately 6,500 journals, plus appropriate monographs, and is currently growing at a rate of about 120,000 citations each year. Subject analysis for these files is somewhat below average because it relies on NAL's *Agricultural/Biological Vocabulary* (about 21,000 terms), which is used to assign an average of five subject headings per record. Some records have none, so others obviously have more than five. Further aids are the NAL call number, based on the Library of Congress classification system, and the use of "enhancement words" or "enrichment terms," as they are variously known, in the title field, in those instances where the title does not adequately indicate the content of the document. Non-English titles are given in the original language or are transliterated, with an English translation. No abstracts are provided.

As with other files generated by the United States government for public availability, *CAIN* represents good value for money: the monthly tapes for the current segment of the file cost $45 per reel, or $540 annually. The backfile to January 1970 is offered at the same rate, and, depending upon the storage density selected, occupies five to eight reels. There are, of course, no royalties or special license agreements necessary.

A modified version of *CAIN* is also available from the Macmillan Information Corporation (formerly CCM Information Corp.) which offers it in the MARC format or in Macmillan Information's own "PX" format, which makes it suitable for searching by programs marketed by the same company.

COMPENDEX (Engineering Index, Incorporated)

*COMP*uterized *EN*gineering In*DEX,* the machine-readable version of *Engineering Index,* the primary abstracting and indexing periodical for the broad discipline of engineering, is available from January 1969 to date. This publication currently provides about 85,000 citations annually from approximately 3,500 journals and from other important sources, such as conference proceedings.

The file comes in TEXT-PAC format, TEXT-PAC being an IBM-produced set of computer programs for free-text searching. Apparently this was the result of a judgment about the general suitability of TEXT-PAC for bibliographic searching, and hence about the number of centers likely to be utilizing it. There is no standard set of programs for performing such searches, although a few years ago it seemed that TEXT-PAC might emerge as that standard among the growing number of search centers then just beginning. This has not in fact happened, but it is reasonable to speculate that such a possibility might have prompted this choice of format; certainly Engineering Index, Incorporated, is not the only tape supplier to offer the file already in the TEXT-PAC format.

COMPENDEX relies for subject specification upon *Engineering Index*'s own *Subject Headings for Engineering* (*SHE*), a controlled vocabulary of some 12,000 terms; in addition to one "main subject heading," records can contain subheadings, as well as free language terms and *SHE* cross-reference terms. The abstract is also part of the tape record.

Tapes are issued monthly, and the cost at present is $6,500 per year for lease (in-house use) and $6,000 per year for license (ability to serve all clients), plus the cost of the physical reels in either case. A sample tape is available, either on loan or for sale at $15, and the backfiles, which begin with 1969, are priced at the same annual rate as the current year's tapes.

COMPENDEX has traditionally been a fairly difficult file to use, primarily because such parts of the record as the subject structure, the various numbers and codes assigned to each citation, and certain other conventions introduce unnecessary complexity into any attempt to search the file efficiently. Obviously it does not help that engineers as a professional group appear to live up to their popular image of being, at best, indifferent users of bibliographic information, and that the production schedule of the file was seriously in arrears during 1972–1973. Given these drawbacks, *COMPENDEX* is a data base which should be considered for acquisition only if one has a very numerous, or a very specialized, user community such as a large university or a major engineering company.

Excerpta Medica (Excerpta Medica Foundation, Amsterdam, The Netherlands)

The Excerpta Medica Foundation originated after World War II as an attempt by practicing physicians to exert better control over the biomedical literature. The cornerstone of its technique was, and still is, to have a scientific paper abstracted and indexed not merely by an information specialist who is academically qualified in the subject concerned, but rather by a biomedical scientist currently working in the specific area which that paper covers. Librarians will recognize behind this practice the familiar "kindred spirit" fallacy. This claims that since only a few people, those kindred spirits working in exactly the same field of research as one's self, can understand the full significance of one's work, therefore only those people can be trusted to assign subject headings, write abstracts, or formulate searches for the bibliographic information in that field. While this is clearly not the case, it does not mean that *Excerpta Medica*'s method does not work—it does; however it is fair to say that the system manifests the disadvantages one would expect, such as a thesaurus containing about 500,000 terms, of which probably half (about 220,000) are preferred terms, or valid descriptors.

Excerpta Medica tapes contain the complete information provided in the forty-two published sections which together comprise *Excerpta Medica*. The massive MALIMET thesaurus (*MA*ster *LI*st of *ME*dical Indexing *Terms*) and the *Excerpta Medica* classification schedules are also available on magnetic tape.

The United States agent for the manipulation of the *Excerpta Medica* tapes, including the performance of searches, was Information Interscience, Incorporated, of Philadelphia, until that company's sudden withdrawal from tape services in late 1972. Until it can make new arrangements, the foundation in Amsterdam is presently handling search requests itself for American clients. The prospective user should be apprised of the charges for this service.[2] For a single-term search (presumably a preferred term), the cost is $175 per profile per year for the first search; $125 for the second; $75 for the third; and $60 for the fourth and all subsequent searches. Multiterm searches, which we have seen to be the more advisable way to employ the computer for literature-searching, are offered at $150 per profile per year for the first one hundred profiles submitted; $120 per profile for the second hundred; $100 per profile for the third hundred; and $75 for the 301st and all subsequent profiles. Retrospective searches back to 1970 are available at the same rates. The file actually extends back to 1968.

For purchase of the tapes, the base fee is $35,000 per year, but this fee is augmented on a sliding scale if any searching for outside clients is performed. The cost of the backfile is also determined according to a sliding scale which ranges from $30,000 for the preceding year, down to approximately $10,000 for 1968. At these rates, it is quite obvious that only those centers with a larger user community (and probably those which are doing biomedical work so advanced that the coverage of the readily available MEDLARS service is inadequate) would be able to afford the purchase of this file.

GEO-REF (American Geological Institute)

GEO-REF (*GEO*logical *RE*ference *File*) is the master data base of the American Geological Institute (AGI); it is used to produce the *Bibliography and Index of Geology*, plus several other specialized bibliographies as well as the annual indexes to twelve primary journals in that field. This last idea is a good one, which many abstracting and indexing services could adopt, though no others yet appear to have done so. Assuming that the essential prerequisite is satisfied, that the journal is abstracted and/or indexed in its entirety, it is now quite likely that one of the major computerized bibliographic services could produce annual or multiyear indexes to a scholarly journal faster and cheaper than the journal publishers could. Essentially, all it would take is a search on the journal title in question, followed by an automatic sorting of the resulting subset by author, keyword, and the like. Since all the major disciplinary services work with a particular core of journals that are given 100 percent coverage, such index production could represent a lucrative spin-off from the main activity.

Input to the *GEO-REF* file is in the order of 40,000 to 50,000 items per year, drawn from 3,000 journals indexed; this makes it the central bibliographic resource in that new grouping of studies known as the earth sciences. However, this is an indexing operation only; no abstracts are provided. Full title is always given, with an English translation for non-English terms, which in fact means approximately 60 percent of the time. In addition to the title, keywords and descriptive phrases are often attached for better subject access. An AGI leaflet (#102) says that "many of the references, whose titles are not fully indicative of the subject matter, are enriched by brief annotative additions," which seems to characterize as an exception what is actually the rule. These "annotative additions" are generally a mixture of keywords and phrases, and consist, in many instances, of two to three lines of information. Unfortunately, it is not merely short items (notes, letters, and the like) which appear without any such annotation; a 59-page paper, the kind that occupies the whole of a journal issue, appeared in the printed bibliography, at least, as an unadorned bibliographic reference. Its title was probably no better and no worse than that of many subject-analyzed entries. In a computerized retrieval operation this practice virtually compels a search of the entire record, since one cannot rely on a search of the subject field alone to recall all the relevant references. The tapes do apparently contain more subject terms than appear in print, but it is not clear whether this means that all tape records have such terms.

The charge for *GEO-REF* tapes is not based on a fixed subscription, but is calculated at 10 cents per reference on the file, which at present implies an annual cost that ranges from $4,200 to $4,800. The royalty fee for provisions of service beyond in-house use is $24 per profile per year for current awareness (SDI) searching, and 10 percent of the charged fee for retrospective searches. Special subsets of the file are available at the same charge of 10 cents per reference, plus a fee of $71.25 for the necessary computer processing. Tapes are issued monthly, and a sample tape is available at no charge. The backfiles to 1966 are also priced at 10 cents per reference, which puts the yearly cost between $1,100 and $3,800, according to size.

Government Reports Announcements
(National Technical Information Service)

The machine-readable version of the National Technical Information Service's *GRA* file was first made available in January 1970, as *U.S. Government Research and Development Reports* (*USGRDR*) from the Clearinghouse for Federal Scientific and Technical Information (CFSTI) as NTIS was then known. At that time, the announcement stated that the backfile to 1967 might be put on tape at a later date. However, the retrospective conversion effort apparently has progressed faster than expected, since issues back to January 1964 are now available. The service, which deals mainly with the research and report literature emanating from the federal government, is adding to its existing file of about 350,000 records at the rate of approximately 60,000 items per year.

Coverage is interdisciplinary, and is arranged in the same sections as the printed version of *Government Reports Announcements,* familiar to many librarians as a prime index to United States government publications on a multitude of topics, from "Education" to "Electronic Countermeasures."

Since the input comes as citations (in an existing bibliographic format) from a variety of government agencies, several of which have their own subject terminology, compatibility has been something of a problem, and a major effort was underway in 1972–73 to rectify the situation. The COSATI list of fields and groups is one scheme used a great deal in the *GRA* file, but AEC, NASA, DDC, as well as other systems also are present. Records may also have "identifiers" or "open-ended terms" added by NTIS indexers, as appropriate. Like ERIC, NTIS has the advantage of being able to provide a backup service with the full document in paper or microfiche format.

The tape subscription is presently $2,000 per year, with previous years available at the same rate. No licensing or royalty arrangements are needed, this being all federal government material in the public domain. Tapes are issued semimonthly, and a sample tape from the current year's issues is available on payment of $25.

INSPEC (Institution of Electrical Engineers, London, England)

INSPEC (*IN*formation *S*ervice in *P*hysics, *E*lectrotechnology and *C*ontrol) is a very large data base with a current input of 150,000 items per year. It covers a distinct, well-defined area not available from any other single source, its printed counterparts being the sum total of *Physics Abstracts, Electrical and Electronics Abstracts,* and *Computer and Control Abstracts.* Furthermore, not only is its pricing quite in keeping with other, comparable, data bases, it also offers a relatively flexible set of acquisition alternatives, its subject control and documentation are both commendable, and it is, in general, what one might term a "good" file.

Yet despite these assets, *INSPEC* is not (as far as the authors can discern) widely used, or even widely known, in the United States, mainly due to the lack of a stable marketing and distribution system. There have been three attempts in the last three years to arrive at a workable arrangement. The first was with a sister organization in this country, the Institute of Electrical and Electronics Engineers, which shortly thereafter decided against becoming involved in the tape supplying business; the second, which also quickly collapsed, was with Information Interscience, Incorporated (3i), of Philadelphia (see *Excerpta Medica*); and the third, which seems to offer more hope of success, began in 1973 when the American Institute of Physics took on the task of marketing *INSPEC* in the United States. This rapid transition from distributor to distributor appears to have been an unfortunate coincidence and not a reflection on the Institution of Electrical Engineers or its data base. It does illustrate, however, the present volatility in the marketing of machine-readable data bases, as various approaches are tried. Librarians and other information specialists with a need to begin offering computerized information services should understand that we are still in the initial phase of data base publication and marketing, and that this phase of experimentation and adjustment will continue for some years to come.

Under the auspices of the American Institute of Physics, two versions of the file are available: *INSPEC–1,* the complete abstracts service; and *INSPEC–2,* a brief "preview" type of listing, which omits the abstract and the document number that refers the user to the printed abstract journal. The reason for this latter omission is not made clear, but it may be because the *INSPEC–2* tape is sent out even before document numbers are assigned. *INSPEC–2* is only available as one complete file, but *INSPEC–1* can be obtained in any of three sections corresponding to the three abstract journals covered, with duplicate records eliminated if the complete edition is chosen. *INSPEC–2* is issued semimonthly, and *INSPEC–1* is issued semimonthly if the subscription comprises or contains the *Physics Abstracts* portion; otherwise it is received monthly. A sample tape is available for $150, credited against "the first full subscription payment" (AIP leaflet) which appears to mean, but may not, that subscribers to anything less than all three sections of *INSPEC–1* would have to pay heavily for the test tape.

The base price ranges from $1,300 per year for the smallest section to $3,900 for all three; to any combination selected must be added a $2,100 service fee before any service at all can be offered, in-house or otherwise. The somewhat flimsy justification for the service fee is that some users may want the tapes "for system and program development or research purposes only" (AIP leaflet). The $2,100 annual service fee allows the subscriber to process 100 current awareness (SDI) profiles and 1,000 retrospective searches. Anything more requires negotiation of an additional charge. Backfiles are available from 1969 on, at prices ranging from $1,300 to $3,900 per year.

Psychological Abstracts (American Psychological Association)

The *Psychological Abstracts* tapes begin with the January 1967 issue. At a current average rate of 24,000 bibliographic citations per year from approximately 800 journals reviewed, *Psychological Abstracts* is not one of the group of "giant" data bases, but it is, nonetheless, potentially a most useful file. This file is the primary resource in its field, and that field is one with wide-ranging cross-disciplinary significance. Unlike the physical and biomedical sciences, from which the leadership in innovative information services has come, the social sciences (and, to an even greater degree, the humanities) are only now beginning to experience the computerization of their bibliographic information on any large scale. *Psychological Abstracts* tapes have, therefore, attracted almost as much interest, in the authors' experience, as have the bigger, established services, *CA-Condensates* and *BA-Previews*.

According to the publicity from *Psychological Abstracts,* tapes are generally offered on a quarterly basis, although they can be supplied monthly or at other frequencies if desired. The lease fee is $3,000 for the current year, $2,000 for the immediately preceding year, and $800 for each year prior to that. License arrangements have not been announced. Until they are, the American Psychological Association will continue to allow any appropriate agency to function as a licensed center at no extra charge, in return for such feedback on usage as will enable an equitable scheme to be worked out. A sample tape is available on a sixty-day loan.

The one insuperable obstacle to acquisition of the tapes in recent months has been that the file is undergoing reorganization for better subject access, resulting in serious slippages in delivery. (At UCLA an order placed in October 1972 had not elicited a single tape by late April 1973 and for that reason had to be cancelled.) One can only hope that the various search services, announced by *Psychological Abstracts* at the same time as were the tapes, are providing better results.

Science Citation Index
(Institute for Scientific Information, Inc.)

The Institute for Scientific Information's *Science Citation Index* has been published since 1964. While it is not our purpose here to discuss in detail the technicalities of citation indexing, a brief outline of the fundamental process may be useful. The reader requiring a fuller treatment of citation indexing principles and methods per se is referred to the excellent article by Weinstock in the *Encyclopedia of Library and Information Science.*[3]

Citation indexing is the indexing of references cited at the end of a scholarly article. As performed by ISI (the company formed by Dr. Eugene Garfield, who is credited with the creation of the first general-purpose citation index), each cited paper becomes a main entry in the citation index, with every author citing it being listed below in alphabetical order. Minimal bibliographic identifying information (essentially, the journal citation) appears with each citing paper. The reader is then referred to a source index for standard bibliographic information about the citing paper. Obviously, one may then use the citing author as a main entry in the citation index, to see who has cited that paper, and thus literally pursue a chain of thought and intellectual influence. Other approaches are made possible by the corporate index and the "Permuterm" subject index, a fully-permuted list of all significant title-words of source items.

Like the printed index, the magnetic tape version of *Science Citation Index* is divided into two parts: the citation file and the source file, which can be purchased separately or together. A lease agreement has also become possible in recent years. We understand the terms of this are to some degree tailored to the client's specific environment, and information is available on request from ISI. The costs of the tapes are: for the citation file, $12,000 for the current year and $6,000 for previous years; for the source file, $8,000 for the current year and $4,000 for previous years. The rate for both is simply the sum of the parts, $20,000 and $12,000 respectively. A reduced rate (half-price) is given to nonprofit organizations for the first year of subscription. It may be of interest to note that the price of the citation file has been reduced substantially since 1968, when it was $24,000, and the combined file $32,000.

Tapes are delivered weekly. The data which they provide are drawn from approximately 2,500 major scientific and technical journals and currently amount to a formidable 84,000 cited references (gathered from approximately 7,000 papers examined) on the average weekly tape.

The principal asset that *Science Citation Index* has to offer is that it successfully fulfills an important bibliographic function not performed anywhere else. It occupies a unique place in the spectrum of bibliographic access to the world's knowledge, and is, in short, a classic example of an idea whose time had come, when Dr. Garfield began to develop it in the late 1950s. By its nature, citation indexing is extremely eclectic, as illustrated by the overall ratio of twelve citations to each article (and incidentally by the appearance among the cited authors of Shakespeare, A. A.

Milne, and other quotable literary figures). Thus, the decision to scan the whole panorama of science was undoubtedly a correct one. It can be argued that the citations an author makes reveal as much about the true significance of his paper as do index terms. This is especially true where an article has an interdisciplinary cast to it; the citations probably pinpoint more accurately than any subject terms the specific nature of the interaction between two different branches of science. Because *Science Citation Index* is the only reference tool of its kind for the sciences, it is a pity that, inclusive as it is, it does not cover a great many more journals, perhaps as many as ten to twelve thousand. Such orders of magnitude cannot shock anyone accustomed to looking at the problems of access to information on a global scale, and as we have stated in previous chapters, this is precisely how computers can and will be utilized increasingly in the future.

One drawback to *Science Citation Index,* and it is a perennial source of irritation to librarian and user alike, is the extremely compacted format. An abbreviated journal title is nothing unusual, but what we get in *SCI* are abbreviations of those abbreviations. Likewise, authors and subject terms are arbitrarily truncated at eleven characters. This is no doubt very pleasing to the computer programmer who takes pride in "tight" coding, which was more important in 1964 when the costs of processing information by computer were indeed higher than they are now. Such compaction, however, greatly increases the probability that one will be compelled to consult a further source, usually another ISI product, to gain sufficient data to work with. A more congenial format for the human eye, regardless of the waste of some space, would be a decided improvement. It is a commonplace that one's receptivity to information is significantly affected by the physical format in which that information is presented.

Bibliography of Data Base Listings

1. Carlson, Gary. *Literary Works in Machine Readable Form.* Provo, Utah: Brigham Young Univ., 1965.
    Updated in the January 1967 issue of *Computers and the Humanities* (*see* item 3 in this list).
2. U.S. National Science Foundation. Office of Scientific Information Service. "Computer-Based Systems," in *Nonconventional Scientific and Technical Information Systems in Current Use.* no. 4. Washington, D.C.: The Foundation, 1966. p. 147–476.
3. *Computers and the Humanities.* New York: Queens College of the City Univ. of New York, 1966– .
    A "Directory of Scholars Active," which appears in this bimonthly journal at irregular intervals, provides a current list of projects under-

way. Many of these projects generate an available machine-readable data base of which brief characteristics are given.

4. Council of Social Science Data Archives. *Social Science Data Archives in the United States, 1967.* New York: The Council, 1967.
5. California. University. Institute of Library Research. *Mechanized Information Service in the University Library: Phase I—Planning.* pt. 3. "Inventory of Available Data Bases," by Joan C. Troutman. Los Angeles: The Institute, 1967.
6. Herner, Saul. *Selected Mechanized Scientific and Technical Information Systems.* Washington, D.C.: Information Resources Pr., 1968.
   Describes 13 systems. Essentially superseded by item 21 in this list.
7. Cohan, Leonard, ed. *Directory of Computerized Information in Science and Technology.* New York: Science Association/International, 1968.
   Updated by irregular and infrequent supplements.
8. Bowles, Edmund A. "Computerized Research in the Humanities: A Survey," in the June 1968 *ACLS Newsletter Special Supplement,* p. 1–49.
9. Science Communication, Inc. *Study of Scientific and Technical Data Activities in the U.S.* Washington, D.C.: NTIS, 1968. 3v. (AD 670 606, AD 670 607, AD 670 608).
10. American Library Association. Science and Technology Reference Services Committee. *A Guide to a Selection of Computer-Based Reference Services in the U.S.A.* Chicago: ALA, 1969.
    A compilation of 54 machine-readable data bases in science and technology and the 18 agencies that produce these files.
11. Hayes, Robert M., and Becker, Joseph. "Inventory of Available Data Bases," in *Handbook of Data Processing for Libraries.* Appendix 3, p. 829–75. New York: Wiley–Becker–Hayes, 1970.
    Lists 48 files, most of which are bibliographic, and is based, in part, on item 5 in this list.
12. Carroll, Kenneth, comp. *Survey of Scientific-Technical Tape Services.* New York: American Institute of Physics and American Society for Information Science, 1970 (AIP ID 70–3; ASSIS SIG/SDI 2).
    Lists 50 commercially available tape services.
13. Kerbec, Matthew J., comp. *Legally Available U.S. Government Information.* 2v. Arlington, Va.: Output Systems Corp. (P.O. Box 2407, Arlington, Va. 22202), 1970. (v.1, NASA; v.2, DOD).
14. Sessions, Vivian S., ed. *Data Bases in the Social and Behavioral Sciences.* New York: Science Associates/International, 1971.
15. Kruzas, Anthony T.; Schnitzer, Anna E.; and Varekamp, Linda E., eds. *Encyclopedia of Information Systems and Services.* Ann Arbor, Mich.: Edwards Bros., 1971.

Access is primarily by name of system or service. Not every responding institution lists a data base, but many of the 833 systems do.

16. Organization for Economic Cooperation and Development, and United
Nations Economic Commission for Europe. *Inventory of Some English-
Language Secondary Information Services in Science and Technology.*
DECD/ECE: 1971.

Cited on p. 6 in item 22 in this list as covering "100 organizations
worldwide providing 141 information systems or services . . . 56 of
these data base producers offer their tapes on a lease or purchase arrangement."

17. Williams, Martha E., and Steward, Alan K. *ASIDIC Survey of Information Center Services.* Chicago: Illinois Institute of Technology
Research Institute, 1972.

Lists on p. 11–16 the services provided by member-organizations of
ASIDIC (Assn. of Scientific Information Dissemination Centers),
which together were processing 48 publicly available data bases.

18. U.S. Dept. of Commerce. National Technical Information Service.
SUMSTAT Catalog. Washington, D.C.: U.S. Dept. of Commerce,
1972–

SUMSTAT (Summary Statistics) is a project to improve access to
publicly available machine-readable summary statistical data files produced by the United States government. This first issue of the
SUMSTAT Catalog, covering the Dept. of Commerce only, lists more
than 100 files from 20 different agencies.

19. Batik, Albert L., and Hale, Eleanor. "ASTM Data Banks and Chemical Information Sources," *Journal of Chemical Documentation* 12(3):
172–74 (Aug. 1972).

Discusses data sources and services available from ASTM (American Society for Testing and Materials), some of which are available
on magnetic tape.

20. *Annual Review of Information Science and Technology.* v.7. Washington, D.C.: American Society for Information Science, 1972. chap. 9.
"Generation and Use of Machine-Readable Bibliographic Data Bases,"
by Marvin Gechman.

21. Herner, Saul, and Vellucci, Matthew J. *Selected Federal Computer-
Based Information Systems.* Washington, D.C.: Information Resources
Pr., 1972.

Enlarged and updated version of item 6 in this list. Consists of 35
system descriptions, several of which produce a publicly available data
base.

22. Schneider, John H.; Gechman, Marvin; and Furth, Stephen E., eds.
Survey of Commercially Available Computer-Readable Bibliographic

Data Bases. Washington, D.C.: American Society for Information Science, Special Interest Group for Selective Dissemination of Information, 1973.

Referred to in the Introduction to this chapter. Provides details of contents and availability of 81 files from 55 suppliers.

23. Patrinostro, Frank S., and Mulherin, Nathan. *Available Data Banks for Library and Information Services.* Tempe, Ariz.: The LARC Assn., 1973.

Provides brief and very limited information on 122 files.

Notes

1. *See* v.1, "General Information and Design Features," in *Chemical Abstracts Service Specifications Manual for Computer-Readable Files in Standard Distribution Format* (Columbus, Ohio: CAS, 1973).
2. The information on charges was provided orally by Mr. B. Stearn of the *Excerpta Medica* Board of Directors.
3. *See* "Citation Indexes," in v.5, *Encyclopedia of Library and Information Science,* Allen Kent and Harold Lancour, eds. (New York: M. Dekker, 1971), p. 16–40.

Appendixes

Appendix A
ERIC Clearinghouses:
Brief Scope Notes

ERIC Clearinghouse on *Adult Education*
Syracuse University
Syracuse, New York

Adult education in public schools, colleges, and universities; activities carried on by national or community voluntary and service agencies; all areas of inservice training; fundamental and literary education for adults; correspondence study; continuing education in the professions.

ERIC Clearinghouse on *Counseling and Personnel Services*
University of Michigan
Ann Arbor, Michigan

Preparation, practice, and supervision of counselors at all educational levels and in all settings; theoretical development of counseling and guidance; use and results of personnel procedures such as testing, interviewing, disseminating, and analyzing such information; group work and case work; nature of pupil, student, and adult characteristics; personnel workers and their relation to career planning, family consultations, and student orientation activities.

ERIC Clearinghouse on *Early Childhood Education*
University of Illinois
Urbana, Illinois

Parental factors, parental behavior; the physical, psychological, social, educational, and cultural development of children from birth through the primary grades; educational theory, research, and practice related to the development of young children.

ERIC Clearinghouse on *Educational Management*
University of Oregon
Eugene, Oregon

Leadership, management, and structure of public and private educational organizations; practice and theory of administration; preservice and in-service preparation of administrators, tasks, and processes of administration; methods and varieties or organization, organizational change, and social context of the organization.

Sites, buildings, and equipment for education; planning, financing, constructing, renovating, equipping, maintaining, operating, insuring, utilizing, and evaluating educational facilities.

ERIC Clearinghouse on *Educational Media and Technology*
Institute for Communication Research
Stanford University
Stanford, California

Individualized instruction, systems approaches, film, television, radio, programmed instruction, computers in education, and miscellaneous audio-visual means of teaching. Technology in instruction and technology in society when clearly relevant to education.

ERIC Clearinghouse on *Exceptional Children*
The Council for Exceptional Children
Arlington, Virginia

Aurally handicapped, visually handicapped, mentally handicapped, physically handicapped, emotionally disturbed, speech handicapped, learning disabilities, and the gifted; behavioral, psychomotor, and communication disorders, administration of special education services; preparation and continuing education of professional and paraprofessional personnel; pre-school learning and development of the exceptional; general studies on creativity.

ERIC Clearinghouse on *Higher Education*
George Washington University
Washington, D.C.

Various subjects relating to college and university students, college and university conditions and problems, college and university programs. Curricular and instructional problems and programs, faculty, institutional research, federal programs, professional education (medical, law, and so on), graduate education, university extension programs, teaching-learning, planning, governance, finance, evaluation, interinstitutional arrangements, and management of higher educational institutions.

ERIC Clearinghouse for *Junior Colleges*
University of California, Los Angeles
Los Angeles, California

Development, administration, and evaluation of public and private community junior colleges. Junior college students, staff, curriculums, programs, libraries, and community services.

ERIC Clearinghouse on *Languages and Linguistics*
Modern Language Association of America
New York, New York

Languages and linguistics. Instructional methodology, psychology of language learning, cultural and intercultural content, application of linguistics, curricular problems and developments, teacher training and qualifications, language sciences, psycho-linguistics, theoretical and applied linguistics, language pedagogy, bilingualism, and commonly and uncommonly taught languages including English for speakers of other languages.

ERIC Clearinghouse on *Library and Information Sciences*
American Society for Information Science
Washington, D.C.

Various detailed aspects of information retrieval, library and information processing, library and information sciences, library services, library and information systems, information utilization, publishing industry, terminology, library facilities and information centers, library materials and equipment, librarian and information science personnel, library organizations, and library education.

ERIC Clearinghouse on *Reading and Communications Skills*
National Council of Teachers of English
Champaign, Illinois

All aspects of reading behavior with emphasis on physiology, psychology, sociology, and teaching. Instructional materials, curricula, tests and measurement, preparation of reading teachers and specialists, and methodology at all levels. Role of libraries and other agencies in fostering and guiding reading. Diagnostic and remedial services in school and clinical settings.

ERIC Clearinghouse on *Rural Education and Small Schools*
New Mexico State University
Las Cruces, New Mexico

Education of Indian Americans, Mexican Americans, Spanish Americans, and migratory farm workers and their children; outdoor education; economic, cultural, social, or other factors related to educational programs in rural areas and small schools; disadvantaged of rural and small school populations.

ERIC Clearinghouse on *Science, Mathematics, and Environmental Education*
Ohio State University
Columbus, Ohio

All levels of science, mathematics, and environmental education; development of curriculum and instructional materials; media applications; impact of interest, intelligence, values, and concept development upon learning; pre-service and in-service teacher education and supervision.

ERIC Clearinghouse for *Social Studies/Social Science Education*
University of Colorado
Boulder, Colorado

All levels of social studies and social science; all activities relating to teachers; content of disciplines; applications of learning theory, curriculum theory, child development theory, and instructional theory; research and development programs; special needs of student groups; education as a social science; social studies/social science and the community.

ERIC Clearinghouse on *Teacher Education*
American Association of Colleges for Teacher Education
Washington, D.C.

School personnel at all levels; all issues from selection through pre-service and in-service preparation and training to retirement; curricula; educational theory and philosophy; general education not specifically covered by Educational Management Clearinghouse; Title XI NDEA Institutes not covered by subject specialty in other ERIC clearinghouses.

ERIC Clearinghouse on *Tests, Measurement, and Evaluation*
Educational Testing Service
Princeton, New Jersey

Tests and other measurement devices; evaluation procedures and techniques; application of tests, measurement, or evaluation in educational projects or programs.

ERIC Clearinghouse on the *Disadvantaged*
Information Retrieval Center on the Disadvantaged
Teachers College
Columbia University
New York, New York

Effects of disadvantaged experiences and environments, from birth onward; academic, intellectual, and social performance of disadvantaged children and youth from grade three through college entrance; programs and practices which provide learning experiences designed to compensate for special problems of disadvantaged; issues, programs, and practices related to economic and ethnic discrimination, segregation, desegregation, and integration in education; issues, programs, and materials related to redressing the curriculum imbalance in the treatment of ethnic minority groups.

ERIC Clearinghouse on *Vocational and Technical Education*
Ohio State University
Columbus, Ohio

Agricultural education, business and office occupations education, distributive education, health occupations education, home economics education, technical education, trade and industrial education, subprofessional fields, industrial arts education, manpower economics, occupational psychology, occupational sociology, and all matters related to the foregoing.

Career Education (an ERIC bibliography)
 Includes citations and abstracts to ERIC documents concerned with the relationship between education and work.

Current Index to Journals in Education
 A monthly current awareness index to more than 600 education and education-related periodicals.

ERIC Descriptor and Identifier Usage Report
 Contains all entries listed for each term in both ERIC data bases, RIE and CIJE.

ERIC Educational Documents Abstracts
 A four-volume set providing ready reference to all reports indexed in RIE from January 1968 through December 1971.

ERIC Educational Documents Index
 Includes references to all research documents in the ERIC collections from 1956 through 1971.

ERIC Information Analysis Products, 1967–1972
 Five-year cumulation of citations and abstracts of those publications which reflect information analysis activities undertaken by the network of ERIC clearinghouses.

ERIC Institution Index
 A two-volume set providing corporate author listings for the research documents in the ERIC collection from 1956 through 1971.

Early Childhood Education (an ERIC bibliography)
 Concerned with the educational, psychological, and cultural development of children from birth through primary grades.

Educational Finance (an ERIC bibliography)
 Includes documents bearing descriptors related to financial aspects of elementary and secondary school programs.

Library and Information Sciences (an ERIC bibliography)
 Lists all accessions in the ERIC collections related to library and information science.

Recent Research in Reading: A Bibliography, 1966–1969
 Includes citations to both the report and journal literature covered by RIE and CIJE.

Research in Education
 A monthly index to research and report literature in education available through the Government Printing Office.

Social Studies and Social Science Education (an ERIC bibliography)
 Includes citations and abstracts of documents relating to curricula, textbooks, research, political attitudes, comparative education and other topics.

Thesaurus of ERIC Descriptors
 The source of all subject headings used for indexing and for retrieval of documents and journals in the ERIC collections.

Appendix C
Statement of Interest Form and Profile

STATEMENT OF INTEREST FORM

CENTER FOR INFORMATION SERVICES
CAMPUS COMPUTING NETWORK
UNIVERSITY OF CALIFORNIA, LOS ANGELES

1. Name (Please print)___J. Ramirez_____ Date ___6/29/72___

2. Position ___Assistant Professor_____ Telephone___X54321___

3. Organization/Department___Graduate School of Education___

4. Address ____123 Moore Hall____

    City ___Campus_____ State _____ Zip_____

5. Individuals who will actually use the service (if different from above):

    Name _____

    Position _____Telephone _____

6. Indicate which data bases are to be searched:

    CA-Condensates   ERIC

        Odd Issues _____   CIJE   X

        Even Issues _____   RIE   X

        Both   _____   Both   _____

    CAIN   _____   OTHER (specify)

    COMPENDEX   _____

        _____   _____

        _____   _____

        _____   _____

7. Type of search requested: ___X___ Current Awareness (SDI)

    _____Retrospective From_____to_____

8. Profile title (short descriptive phrase):_____

    Early Childhood Education
    _____

9. Please describe in your own words the subject in which you are interested and on which you want references. Be specific, and define
   terms which have special meaning in your request. If certain facets
   of the subject are not of interest to you, explicitly state that they
   are to be excluded.

    _____ I am interested in information related to the _____

    _____ design and/or evaluation of programs for _____

    _____ "Disadvantaged" children in their early _____

    _____ childhood education. _____

    _____

    _____

    _____

    _____

    _____

    _____

    _____

    _____

    _____

    _____

    _____

    _____

    _____

    _____

    _____

    _____

10. List the important terms (words and word phrases) in your statement
    of interest and any synonyms or special uses you wish to exclude.
    Be sure to include both scientific and common terms. Your careful
    completion of this table will help to refine the profile.

TERMS	SYNONYMS, CLOSELY RELATED TERMS	EXCLUDED USES
Disadvantaged children	bilingual students, Mexican	
	Americans, Spanish speaking,	
	bilingualism	
early childhood education	elementary school students,	
	pre-school education,	
	primary grades, primary	
	education, elementary	
	grades, kindergarten children	
educational programs	bilingual education, compensatory	
	educational programs, pre-school	
	programs	

11. List any particular authors whose writing always interest you
     (specify first and middle names, if possible):

     Lilian Katz, Constance Kamii
     _____

     Bettye Caldwell, Ellis Evans, Courtney Cazden
     _____

     _____

12. List any journals or other periodicals which you regularly read and
     of whose contents you do not need to be informed:

     Young Children
     _____

     Educational Leadership
     _____

     _____

13. Check any of the following types of references that you do <u>not</u> want
     to receive:

     patents   _____   technical papers   _____

     dissertations   _____   books   _____

     conference
     proceedings   _____   periodical articles   _____

14. Do you wish to receive references to documents written in

     _____ English   _____ any language

     _____ other languages (specify) _____

15. Do you wish to receive

     _____X_____ nearly all possibly relevant references

     _____ fewer, very probably relevant references

16. What is the maximum number of references you would wish to receive in any one weekly run? 50

17. List one or two references in your **area** of interest that you have recently found useful.

    E. Evans, Contemporary Influences in Early Childhood Education,

    Holt, Rinehart & Winston, New York, 1971, 366p.

    _____

    _____

<u>PROFILE</u>

EARLY CHILDHOOD EDUCATION

ERC150 1S	J RAMIREZ
ERC150 TITLE	EARLY CHILDHOOD EDUCATION
ERC150 A1	DISADVANTAGED ADJ CHILDREN
ERC150 A2	BILINGUAL ADJ STUDENTS OR EDUCATION
ERC150 A3	MEXICAN ADJ AMERICANS
ERC150 A4	SPANISH ADJ SPEAKING
ERC150 A5	BILINGUALISM
ERC150 ASUM	A1 OR A2 OR A3 OR A4 OR A5
ERC150 B1	EARLY ADJ CHILDHOOD ADJ EDUCATION
ERC150 B2	PRIMARY ADJ SCHOOLS* OR EDUCATION
ERC150 B3	PRIMARY OR ELEMENTARY ADJ GRADES
ERC150 B4	CHILDREN WITH KINDERGARTEN
ERC150 BSUM	B1 OR B2 OR B3 OR B4
ERC150 CSUM	PROGRAM CONTROL50 ADJ DESIGN OR EVALUATION
ERC150 CON1	ASUM AND BSUM AND CSUM
ERC150 CON2	KATZ CONTROL10 ,20 ADJ LILIAN
ERC150 CON3	CALDWELL CONTROL10 ,20 ADJ BETTYE
ERC150 CON4	EVANS CONTROL10 ,20 ADJ ELLIS
ERC150 CON5	KAMII CONTROL10 ,20 ADJ CONSTANCE
ERC150 CON6	CAZDEN CONTROL10 ,20 ADJ COURTNEY
ERC150 CON7	NOT YOUNG CONTROL40 ADJ COURTNEY
ERC150 CON8	NOT EDUCATIONAL CONTROL40 ADJ LEADERSHIP

Appendix D
Some MARC Processing Centers

Approximately sixty organizations, more than a quarter of them outside the United States, are now subscribing to MARC tapes. The majority of these agencies are libraries serving nations, states, parliaments, colleges, universities, counties, cities, government departments, armed forces, and research institutes. In addition, book dealers, bibliographic centers, and information-marketing companies are utilizing MARC data for an ever-expanding clientele.

The following is a list of organizations presently supplying some form of service from MARC tapes to other organizations.

Richard Abel & Co.
P.O. Box 4245
Portland, OR 97201

Autocomp, Inc.
7910 Woodmont Ave.
Bethesda, MD 20014

The Baker & Taylor Co.
50 Kirby Ave.
Somerville, NJ 08876

R. R. Bowker Co.
1180 Avenue of the Americas
New York, NY 10036

The British National Bibliography
7 Rathbone St.
London W 1, England

Computext
15 Charles St., 7–C
New York, NY 10114

Information Design, Inc.
3247 Middlefield Rd.
Menlo Park, CA 94025

Information Dynamics Corp.
80 Main St.
Reading, MA 01867

Inforonics, Inc.
147 Main St.
Maynard, MA 01754

Lehigh University
Lindermann Library
Bethlehem, PA 18015

Macmillan Information
866 Third Ave.
New York, NY 10022

National Library of Australia
Canberra, ACT 2606, Australia

National Science Library of Canada
National Research Council
100 Sussex Dr.
Ottawa 7, ON, Canada

North Carolina State University
D. H. Hills Library
Raleigh, NC 27607

Ohio College Library Center
1314 Kinnear Rd.
Columbus, OH 43212

Oklahoma Dept. of Libraries
109 State Capitol
Oklahoma City, OK 73105

Products of Information Systems
225 Paularino Ave.
Costa Mesa, CA 92627

The Science Press, Inc.
300 West Chestnut St.
Ephrata, PA 17522

University of Florida
University Library
Gainesville, FL 32601

University of Massachusetts
University Library
Amherst, MA 01002

University of Toronto
University Library
Toronto 181, ON, Canada

Xerox Bibliographics
2500 Schuster Dr.
Cheverly, MD 20781

Recognizing the national need to stimulate public utilization of the 1970 Census in machine-readable form, the Center for Research Libraries has hastened the development of a Census Laboratory and Clearinghouse. This is currently operated by DUALabs (National Data Use and Access Laboratories) of 1601 North Kent Street, Rosslyn, Virginia, 22209, and includes a nationwide system of User Contact Sites, several of them libraries, at which researchers needing access to the machine-readable census may find out about the data held and the services offered by each of the sites, and centrally by DUALabs. An important feature of the program is the emphasis on user orientation. Below are the agencies presently designated as User Contact Sites of the Census Laboratory and Clearinghouse.

Concordia Teachers College
Center for Social Research in the
  Church
7400 Augusta St.
River Forest, IL 60305

Illinois State University
Department of Sociology-Anthro-
  pology
Normal, IL 61761

The Kroger Company
1014 Vine St.
Cincinnati, OH 45201

Massachusetts Institute of Technology
UNITEL Census Program
The MIT Libraries
Cambridge, MA 02139

Metropolitan Planning Commission
of Nashville and Davidson
County
Metropolitan Office Bldg.
P.O. Box 39
Nashville, TN 37202

Pennsylvania State University
Computation Center
University Park, PA 16802

Princeton-Rutgers Census Data
Project
Princeton University Computer
Center
87 Prospect Ave.
Princeton, NJ 08540

Texas A & M University
University Library
College Station, TX 77843

University of California, Los Angeles
University Research Library,
Public Affairs Service
405 Hilgard Ave.
Los Angeles, CA 90024

University of Florida
University Libraries
Library West
Gainesville, FL 32601

University of Houston
Cullen College of Engineering
Houston, TX 77004

University of Mississippi
Institute of Urban Research
University, MS 38677

University of Missouri
Demographic Data Service
Sociology Bldg.
Columbia, MO 65201

University of North Carolina
Social Science Data Library
Institute for Research in Social
Science
Chapel Hill, NC 27514

Selected Bibliography

"All about ERIC," *Journal of Educational Data Processing* 7:51–129 (Apr. 1970).

Anglo-American Cataloging Rules. Chicago: American Library Assn., 1967. 400p.

Artandi, Susan. *An Introduction to Computers in Information Science.* 2d ed. Metuchen, N.J.: Scarecrow, 1972.

Automation and the Library of Congress ("The King Report"). Washington, D.C.: Library of Congress, 1963.

Barhydt, Gordon C., and Schmidt, Charles T. *Information Retrieval Thesaurus of Education Terms.* Cleveland, Ohio: The Press of Case Western Reserve University, 1968. 133p.

Brandhorst, W. Ted. "ERIC Improving Education—That's What It's All About." *The LEASCO Magazine* 2:27–30 (Jan./Feb. 1971).

Bundy, Mary Lee. "Automation as Innovation." *Drexel Library Quarterly* 4:317–28 (Oct. 1968).

Bushnell, Don D., and Allen, Dwight W., eds. *The Computer in American Education.* New York: Wiley, 1967.

Carroll, Kenneth D. *Survey of Scientific-Technical Tape Services.* New York: American Institute of Physics, 1970.

Cleverdon, Cyril W. *Factors Determining the Performance of Indexing Systems.* 2 vols. Cranfield, England: College of Aeronautics, 1966.

Cohen, M., and Nagel, E. *An Introduction to Logic and Scientific Method.* New York: Harcourt, 1934.

Copi, Irving M. *Introduction to Logic.* 3d ed. New York: Macmillan, 1968.

COSATI Standard for Descriptive Cataloging of Government Scientific and Technical Reports. Springfield, Va.: National Technical Information Service, 1966. 50p.

Cox, N. S. M., Dews, J. D., and Dolby, J. L. *The Computer and the Library.* Hamden, Conn.: Shoe String, Archon Books, 1967.

Elias, Arthur W., ed. *Key Papers in Information Science.* Washington, D.C.: American Society for Information Science, 1971.

ERIC Clearinghouse Scope of Interest Manual. Bethesda, Md.: ERIC Processing and Reference Facility, LEASCO Systems and Research Corp., 1971. Unnumb.

ERIC Operating Manual, Section 3. Bethesda, Md.: ERIC Processing and Reference Facility, LEASCO Systems and Research Corporation, 1971. Parts numbered separately.

Farr, Richard S. *Knowledge Linkers and the Flow of Educational Information.* Stanford, Calif.: ERIC Clearinghouse on Educational Media and Technology, 1969. 14p.

Format Recognition Process for MARC Records: A Logical Design. Report on a project partially sponsored by the U.S. Office of Education, conducted by the Information Systems Office, Library of Congress. Chicago: American Library Assn., Information Science and Automation Division, 1970.

Foskett, A. C. *The Subject Approach to Information.* Hamden, Conn.: Shoe String, Archon Books, 1969. 310p.

Foskett, D. J. "A Note on the Concept of Relevance." *Information Storage and Retrieval* 8:77 (Apr. 1972).

Gardner, Martin. *Logic Machines and Diagrams.* New York: McGraw-Hill, 1958.

Goodman, Frederick. "The Role and Function of the Thesaurus in Education." In *Thesaurus of ERIC Descriptors.* New York: Macmillan Information, 1972.

Harris, Jessica Lee. *Subject Analysis: Computer Implications of Rigorous Definition.* Metuchen, N.J.: Scarecrow, 1970. 279p.

Hayes, Robert M., and Becker, Joseph. *Handbook of Data Processing.* New York: Wiley, 1971. 885p.

Henley, J. P. *Computer-based Library and Information Systems.* 2d ed. London: Macdonald; and New York: American Elsevier, 1972.

Jahoda, Gerald. *Information Storage and Retrieval Systems for Individual Researchers.* New York: Wiley, 1970. 135p.

Kalish, D., and Montague, R. *Logic: Techniques of Formal Reasoning.* New York: Harcourt, 1964.

Kaplan, Louis, ed. *Reader in Library Services and the Computer.* Washington, D.C.: NCR Microcard Editions, 1971.

Kemeny, John G.; Snell, J. Laurie; and Thompson, Gerald L. *Introduction to Finite Mathematics.* 2d ed. Englewood Cliffs, N.J.: Prentice-Hall, 1966.

Kline, Morris. *Mathematics for Liberal Arts.* Reading, Mass.: Addison-Wesley, 1967.

Knight, G. Norman, ed. *Training in Indexing: A Course of the Society of Indexers.* Cambridge, Mass.: The M.I.T. Press, 1969. 219p.

Lancaster, F. Wilfrid. *Information Retrieval Systems; Characteristics, Testing, and Evaluation.* New York: Wiley, 1968.

Landry, Bertrand Clovis. *A Theory of Indexing: Indexing Theory as a Model for Information Storage and Retrieval.* Washington, D.C.: National Science Foundation, Office of Science Information Service, 1971. 282p. (ED 057 843).

Licklider, J. C. R. *Libraries of the Future.* Cambridge, Mass.: The M.I.T. Press, 1965.

Luhn, Hans Peter. "A Business Intelligence System." *IBM Journal of Research and Development* 2(4):314–19 (Oct. 1958).

McAllister, Caryl. *A Study and Model of Machine-Like Indexing Behavior by Human Indexers.* Los Gatos, Calif.: Advanced Systems Development Division, International Business Machines Corporation, 1971. 146p. (ED 056 736).

MARC Manuals Used by the Library of Congress. 2d ed. Prepared by the Information Systems Office, Library of Congress. Chicago: American Library Assn., Information Science and Automation Division, 1970.

MARC Pilot Project. (Final Report on a project sponsored by the Council on Library Resources, Inc.) Prepared by Henriette D. Avram, Project Director. Washington, D.C.: Library of Congress, 1968.

Marron, Harvey, and Sullivan, Patricia. "Information Dissemination in Education: A Status Report." *College and Research Libraries* 32:286–94 (July 1971).

Massey, Gerald J. *Understanding Symbolic Logic.* New York: Harper, 1970.

Mathies, Lorraine. "The Educational Resources Information Center." *Journal of Educational Data Processing* 7:123–29 (Apr. 1970).

1970 Census Users' Guide. Parts I and II. Washington, D.C.: U.S. Dept. of Commerce, Bureau of the Census, 1970.

Sears List of Subject Headings. 9th ed. New York: Wilson, 1965.

Sharp, John R. *Some Fundamentals of Information Retrieval.* London: Andre Deutsch, 1965. 224p.

———— *Information Retrieval: Notes for Students.* (Grafton Basic Texts) London: Andre Deutsch, 1970.

Shera, Jesse H. *Documentation and the Organization of Knowledge.* Hamden, Conn.: Shoe String, Archon Books, 1966. 185p.

Thesaurus of ERIC Descriptors. 4th ed. New York: Macmillan Information, 1972. 330p.

U.S. Office of Education. Panel on Educational Terminology. *Rules for Thesaurus Preparation.* 2d ed. Washington, D.C.: Govt. Print. Off., 1966.

Vickery, Brian C. *Techniques of Information Retrieval.* Hamden, Conn.: Shoe String, Archon Books, 1970.

Watson, Peter G., and Briggs, R. Bruce. "Computerized Information Services for the University Community." *Information Storage and Retrieval* 8(1):21–33 (Feb. 1972).

Index

This index is arranged in letter-by-letter order throughout all entries, e.g., ALA, American.

Entries are given for unofficial titles and acronyms with cross-references to the specific entries, e.g., ERIC Thesaurus, *see Thesaurus of ERIC Descriptors,* or, MARC, *see* Machine-Readable Cataloging.